NATURE'S KINDRED SPIRITS

Nature's Kindred Spirits

ALDO LEOPOLD,
JOSEPH WOOD KRUTCH,
EDWARD ABBEY, ANNIE DILLARD,
AND GARY SNYDER

James I. McClintock

The University of Wisconsin Press

The University of Wisconsin Press
114 North Murray Street
Madison, Wisconsin 53715

3 Henrietta Street
London WC2E 8LU, England

Library of Congress Cataloging-in-Publication Data
McClintock, James, I., 1939–
    Nature's kindred spirits: Aldo Leopold, Joseph Wood Krutch,
 Edward Abbey, Annie Dillard, and Gary Snyder / James I. McClintock.
    200 p.   cm.
    Includes bibliographical references (p. 163) and index.
    ISBN 0-299-14170-5 (cl.).   ISBN 0-299-14174-8 (pb.)
    1. American literature—20th century—History and criticism.
 2. Natural history—United States—History—20th century.
 3. Nature in literature.   I. Title.
 PS228.N39M37   1994
 818'.54080936—dc20   93-38110

For Will, Matt, Sally, and Jim

Contents

Acknowledgments

I am grateful for the generous financial support I have received from the National Endowment for the Humanities and Michigan State University; I could not have completed the project without it. I owe a scholarly debt to colleagues and students in Michigan State University's American Studies Program, English Department, and Science-Technology Studies Program in Lyman Briggs School. I especially thank Professors Reed Baird, Bruce Curtis, Victor Howard, Philip Korth, and David Wright for their intellectual companionship and critical attention to various drafts of the manuscript. Additional important help came from Howard Anderson, William Barillas, Tom Blues, Richard Divelbiss, John Kinch, Rod Phillips, Bob Smith, Katarzyna Tomkiewicz, and Bill Wilson. My wife, Sally (an educator), my sons Matt and Will (an artist and a biologist), and my father (a biologist) contributed more than they realize. It has been a joy to find this work uniting us in ways I had not anticipated.

Versions of parts of Chapters 3, 5, and 6 appeared in *Journal of American Culture, Cithera,* and *The American Biology Teacher.* A version of Chapter 4 appeared in *Critique* 31 (Fall, 1989): 41–54. Reprinted with permission of the Helen Dwight Reid Educational Foundation. Published by Heldref Publications, 1319 18th Street, N.W., Washington, D.C. 20036–1802. Copyright 1989.

The wood engravings are by Matthew W. McClintock.

Abbreviations

AL	*Aldo Leopold: His Life and Work* (Curt Meine)
AR	*Abbey's Road* (Edward Abbey)
CP	*Collected Poems 1957-1982* (Wendell Berry)
CSCA	*Companion to* A Sand County Almanac (J. Baird Callicott, ed.)
DR	*Down the River* (Edward Abbey)
DS	*Desert Solitaire* (Edward Abbey)
EPB	*Essays in Philosophical Biology* (William Morton Wheeler)
GANW	*Great American Nature Writing* (Joseph Wood Krutch)
JH	*The Journey Home* (Edward Abbey)
MLO	*More Lives Than One* (Joseph Wood Krutch)
NE	*Nature's Economy* (Donald Worster)
OL	*One Life at a Time, Please* (Edward Abbey)
OW	*The Old Ways* (Gary Snyder)
PTC	*Pilgrim at Tinker Creek* (Annie Dillard)
PW	*The Practice of the Wild* (Gary Snyder)
RM	*Resist Much, Obey Little* (James Hepworth and Gregory McNamee, eds.)
RMG	*The River of the Mother of God and Other Essays by Aldo Leopold* (Susan Flader and J. Baird Callicott, eds.)
RN	*The Rights of Nature* (Roderick Nash)
RW	*The Real Work: Interviews and Talks 1964-1979* (Gary Snyder)
SCA	*A Sand County Almanac: With Essays on Conservation from Round River* (Aldo Leopold)
TI	*Turtle Island* (Gary Snyder)
VD	*The Voice of the Desert* (Joseph Wood Krutch)

Introduction

Contemporary American writers who derive their deepest insights from experiences in nature are not well understood, partly because academics have slighted their works—popular interest has superceded critical attention. There are signs, however, that scholars will no longer neglect them. More than forty years since Joseph Wood Krutch outlined the history and conventions of nature essays in the lengthy and important prologue to his anthology, *Great American Nature Writing* (1950), excellent anthologies of nature writing are appearing once more. Four of note are *The Norton Book of Nature Writing* (1990), edited by Robert Finch and John Elder; *This Incomperable Lande: A Book of American Nature Writing* (1989), edited by Thomas J. Lyon; *Words from the Land: Encounters with Natural History Writing* (1988), edited by Stephen Trimble; and *On Nature: Nature, Landscape, and Natural History* (1987), edited by Daniel Halpern.

   The Norton Book of Nature Writing represents the nature-writing tradition in English-speaking countries other than just the United States. Selections begin with excerpts from Englishman Gilbert White's eighteenth-century essays and conclude with works by more than three dozen contemporary writers, mostly Americans. These post-1945 American writers, who have rarely received critical attention individually or in the aggregate, include Ann Zwinger, Richard Selzer, Ursula K. Le Guin, John McPhee, Chet Raymo, Robert Finch, David Wallace, Gretel Ehrlich, Robert Pyle, David Quammen, Gary Paul Nabhan, and Terry Williams.

   This Incomperable Lande begins with a ninety-page history of nature writing, including a sketch of contemporary writing. Lyon emphasizes that writers have had to absorb and respond to a radical increase in scientific research. The volume's substantial annotated bibliography of primary and secondary sources is the best available. In addition to excerpts from books by Joseph Wood Krutch, Annie Dillard, and Edward Abbey, Lyon includes selections from Rachel Carson, Peter Matthiessen, Edward Hoagland, Wendell Berry, John Haines, Barry Lopez, and John Hay.

Words from the Land is the only anthology devoted exclusively to contemporary essays. Drawing upon interviews he had with fifteen writers of natural history, Trimble introduces them by emphasizing their research and writing methods as well as their positive sense of community with one another and common sense of moral concern. The writers he interviewed include Gretel Ehrlich, Robert Finch, John Hay, Barry Lopez, John Madson, John McPhee, Gary Nabhan, David Quammen, and Ann Zwinger.

On Nature includes nature essays by a number of the writers included in the other anthologies as well as essays more broadly about nature and nature writing by such well-known mainstream literary figures as Italo Calvino, Leslie Marmon Silko, Joyce Carol Oates, and John Fowles. The volume concludes with an annotated bibliography of books on natural history selected by nature writers who served as the volume's advisory editors: Annie Dillard, Gretel Ehrlich, Robert Finch, John Hay, Edward Hoagland, and Barry Lopez. A substantial bibliography of "American Nature Writing" compiled by Thomas J. Lyon concludes the collection.

These four anthologies do a service in bringing the writers to our attention in a fashion that invites critical readings. Contemporary American nature writers, however, have received almost no extended study. Only four books surveying such authors are noteworthy. John Elder's *Imagining the Earth: Poetry and the Vision of Nature* (1985) is an eloquent examination of poetry by, among others, Gary Snyder, A. R. Ammons, Wendell Berry, and Denise Levertov, as well as prose by Annie Dillard and Peter Matthiessen. Peter A. Fritzell's *Nature Writing and America: Essays upon a Cultural Type* (1990) is an ambitious work that presents a history of American nature writing with examples of extended deconstructionist readings of works by Thoreau, Leopold, and Dillard. Sherman Paul in *For the Love of the*

World: Essays on Nature Writers (1992), while arguing no overarching thesis, discusses with brilliance and charm a wide range of essays by Henry David Thoreau, John Muir, Aldo Leopold, Henry Beston, Loren Eiseley, Richard Nelson, and Barry Lopez. Finally, Scott Slovic, in *Seeking Awareness in American Nature Writing: Henry Thoreau, Annie Dillard, Edward Abbey, Wendell Berry, Barry Lopez* (1992), argues the thesis that nature writers "are not merely, or even primarily, analysts of nature or appreciators of nature—rather, they are students of the human mind, literary psychologists" (3).

Of individual writers, only Aldo Leopold and Gary Snyder are receiving sustained study. After initial attention in Roderick Nash's pioneering *Wilderness and the American Mind* (1967), Leopold's life and work have been subjects of four important books: Susan Flader's study of his developing ecological attitudes, *Thinking like a Mountain* (1974); J. Baird Callicott's *Companion to* A Sand County Almanac (1987); Curt Meine's superb biography, *Aldo Leopold: His Life and Work* (1988); and a volume of Leopold's previously uncollected essays edited and perceptively introduced by Susan Flader and J. Baird Callicott, *The River of the Mother of God and Other Essays by Aldo Leopold* (1991). That Leopold's life and work probably will continue to anchor new scholarly studies of attitudes toward nature is suggested by the chapter Max Oelschlaeger devotes to him in *The Idea of Wilderness from Prehistory to the Age of Ecology* (1991).

Since his poetry came to the attention of literary critics in the early 1960s, Gary Snyder has received steady attention from such important literary scholars as Charles Altieri, Richard Howard, Thomas Lyon, Thomas Parkinson, and Sherman Paul. There are four longer studies: Bob Steuding's *Gary Snyder* (1976), Charles Molesworth's *Gary Snyder's Vision: Poetry and the Real Work* (1983), Tim Dean's *Gary Snyder and the American Unconscious: Inhabiting the Ground* (1991), and Patrick D. Murphy's *Understanding Gary Snyder* (1992). A valuable but nonscholarly volume devoted to Snyder's life and work is *Gary Snyder: Dimensions of a Life* (1991), edited by Jon Halper and containing essays by Snyder's friends, among whom are many familiar to anyone who takes an interest in nature writing and environmental matters: Wendell Berry, Richard Nelson, Dave Fore-

man, George Sessions, Peter Berg, Wes Jackson, Michael Mc-
Clure, and Jerome Rothenberg.

In the past two decades, fundamental historical studies of
American attitudes toward nature have set the stage for closer
study of the many more individual writers deserving scholarly
attention. Preceded by Nash's *Wilderness and the American Mind*,
they include Nash's own *The Rights of Nature* (1989), Donald
Worster's *Nature's Economy: The Roots of Ecology* (1977), Paul
Brooks's *Speaking for Nature: How Literary Naturalists from Henry
David Thoreau to Rachel Carson Have Shaped America* (1980),
Stephen Fox's *John Muir and His Legacy: The American Conservation Movement* (1981), and Oelschlaeger's *Idea of Wilderness*.

While I hope my work will be of interest to those studying
the nature essay and the history of American attitudes toward
nature, I am not concerned solely with the nature essay nor am
I writing history. This book is for readers drawn to these essays, poems, and fiction because individually and collectively
the literature, based upon experience in nature and written in
the last half of the twentieth century, offers a critique of modernity and a positive vision. Absorbed in seeing and understanding the natural world close at hand, Aldo Leopold, Joseph
Wood Krutch, Edward Abbey, Annie Dillard, and Gary Snyder
constitute a community of interest by sharing a cluster of ideas
and values that arise from their intense relations with nature
and which, while consistent with what they know about science, are political, philosophical, and religious. Because of their
experiences with nature, they have undergone profound re-
newals in the ways they embrace life, and each has expressed
that renewal aesthetically. Their essays, stories, and poems
sustain a vision of contemporary possibilities that counters
mainstream pessimism, fragmented sensibility, politics of self-
interest, and spiritual confusion. Running counter to the main
literary tradition represented at first by Ernest Hemingway and
lately by Thomas Pynchon, they intuit that our knowledge of
nature, our social arrangements, and our spiritual conditions
can be integrated positively.

While I might have selected any of the two dozen or more
writers I have already mentioned, I have selected five who, for
me, have been the most fascinating in terms of their individual

work as well as in revealing the lines of similarity and difference that link contemporary Americans writing about nature or, more accurately, writing about many subjects after having prepared themselves with solitary experiences in nature. Leopold (1877–1948), arguably the century's foremost conservationist, understood nature from a post-Darwinian ecological perspective that led him to speculate hopefully about an ethical basis for positive individual and social relationships to the land. His classic *A Sand County Almanac* (1949) employs the nature essay genre to sketch the dynamics of environmental history and to teach fundamental ecological ideas. Joseph Wood Krutch (1893–1970), Columbia University English professor and drama critic for *The Nation*, converted from modernist despair to a joyous pantheism he found consistent with scientific thought, even as he turned to nature writing and popularized Leopold's ethic and principles of conservation. Edward Abbey (1927–1989), who identified himself closely with Jack London and his dark world view, used a desert backdrop for finding "antidotes to despair." He adopted the "biocentric" perspective popularized by Leopold and Krutch that human beings are no more special than other living beings and made that viewpoint a basis for political action. Annie Dillard (b. 1945), author most notably of *Pilgrim at Tinker Creek* (1974), is fascinated with even the smallest natural event and, simultaneously, is preoccupied with spiritual renewal. Haunted by the horrors she has witnessed in nature and doubting central Christian tenets, she ransacks her experiences in nature and with religion to find the elements necessary for affirmation. Finally, Gary Snyder (b. 1930), one of America's most important living poets and an insightful critic of American values and behaviors, has fully articulated a powerful ecological vision of harmony among nature, society, and the spirit.

The order I have chosen to present these five figures is somewhat arbitrary since one can construct rationales for other sequences. Any rationale, however, would probably place Aldo Leopold first. He came of age in the twenties and died shortly after World War II, a lifetime that parallels the coming of age of the ecological sciences. As a conservationist, he introduced ecological thinking to conservation practices and policies; as a teacher, he educated a generation of influential wild-life ecologists. Leopold is often called the "prophet" of environmentalism and is thought of as its philosopher. Without question, *A Sand County Almanac*, especially its essay "The Land Ethic," directly and indirectly shaped popular attitudes and rhetoric about environmental reform.

After Leopold I present Joseph Wood Krutch, also of the prewar generation. His intellectual disposition was formed by the great humanistic debates at the turn of the century occasioned by Darwinism, Marxism, and Freudianism. But he became a disciple of Leopold and wrote about nature and in defense of the natural environment during the 1950s and 1960s, the two decades following Leopold's death. His early work defines the modernist world view as alienating, but his writing about joyful experiences in nature exhibits a pattern found in the work of the other writers.

Edward Abbey follows Krutch because he is in the next generation and because his fundamental outlook is close to Krutch's. An agnosticism forged in turn-of-the century scientism characterizes Abbey's spiritual position. Moreover, he derives his emotional associations with nature from his literary predecessors Jack London, Robinson Jeffers, and B. Traven. That means they are darker, more Darwinian than the other writers' associations, aligning as much with a modernist temperament as with the more cheerful views espoused by Dillard and Snyder.

Annie Dillard, the youngest in the group, is the most subjective and the least political but the most like Thoreau in her extravagant language and the intensity of her spiritual pilgrimage. I could just as well have begun or concluded my study with her work. But it is more appropriate to conclude with Snyder since the most important elements of all the others' work appear in his: Leopold's ethic and sense of place, Krutch's incorporation of science into a broader vision of nature and society, Abbey's self-conscious literary heritage and political indignation, and Dillard's faithful spiritual pilgrimage and mystical experience.

Despite their differences—Snyder doesn't write nature essays in the natural history tradition, Dillard is silent on environmental issues, Abbey doesn't use scientific texts, and so on—they constitute an informal community of concern and experience. In particular, as I have noted, Krutch built his arguments on a foundation Aldo Leopold had left him; one of the last interviews Krutch granted was to journalist-admirer Edward Abbey; Abbey praises Dillard as the contemporary most true to Thoreau's example; and Snyder engaged in friendly sparring with Abbey over the value of Buddhism and then found common ground in the necessity for radical action in the environmental movement.

More broadly and importantly, the five writers are alike in their preoccupations with nature, insisting that their experiences in nature inform and be consistent with their other views, whether scientific, political, or spiritual. This insistence on seeing it whole, on consistency between the parts and the whole, between experience and thought, between principle and conduct, and between knowledge and daily life marks them apart from the main currents of twentieth-century literary and social thinking that have most attracted critics and historians.

NATURE'S KINDRED SPIRITS

1
Kindred Spirits

The simplest and most lumpish fungus [is] related to ourselves.
—Henry David Thoreau (1854)

ECOLOGY: The branch of biology that deals with interrelationships.
—Donald Worster (1977)

One way to think about Aldo Leopold, Joseph Wood Krutch, Edward Abbey, Annie Dillard, and Gary Snyder as a group is that they have integrated Thoreauvian Romanticism and twentieth-century ecological biology. While Darwinian science and the early conservation movement had been inimical to the Romantic veneration of nature, mid-twentieth-century ecology offered to restore compatibility between human and nonhuman nature. The scientific and literary Darwinian view of nature as violent, irrational, and wasteful led conservationists to emphasize an anthropocentric philosophy of rational control over nature for human ends. But post-Darwinian ecological studies describe a more benign nature kept stable through complex networks of interdependent organisms. Cooperation as well as competition, interrelationships as well as individualism, harmony as well as strife are features of natural processes. Ecology encourages a biocentric perspective that emphasizes kinship, even equality, between humans and other forms of life. Its compatibility with a Romantic outlook is striking.

The most recent students of American nature essays argue convincingly that the characterizing features of the genre are Romantic attributes combined with science. In his overview of the history of nature writing, *This Incomperable Lande*, Thomas Lyon claims that

> many of the values seen in nature writing are shared with Romanticism: affirmation of the world as congenial to man, in es-

3

sence; skepticism toward purely rationalistic (that is, logical and
sequential, as opposed to intuitive) thought; scorn for materialism; love for what is spontaneous, fecund, and life-giving; and a
predilection for the simple and primitive. (20)

But, he continues, "nature writing is not simply Romantic; it
also owes much to science," both its information and its theories. Similarly, in *Nature Writing and America*, Peter Fritzell
points to *Walden* as the defining text and *Walden*'s defining
qualities as "coordinate obsessions" with "the peculiarities of
personal condition and experience" (the self) and "a scientifically rendered nonhuman nature" (77). The most important
works in this genre, according to Fritzell, exhibit a

> rather unusual combination of intense personal "narrative," a di-
> alectic amalgam of self-analysis and self-reflection (if not self-cel-
> ebration), on the one hand, and extensive, impersonal scientific
> description and explication, on the other—a combination that
> characteristically accompanies (and no doubt at least partly pro-
> vokes) a distinct philosophical (epistemological and metaphysi-
> cal) bent. (73)

Leopold, Krutch, Abbey, Dillard, and Snyder have all, in
varying degrees, combined their Thoreauvian intuitions and
loyalties with modern, post-Darwinian science. Henry David
Thoreau is crucial to each of these writers. Aldo Leopold identifies Thoreau, along with John Muir and John Burroughs, as
his own literary companions who understood that nature's
creatures are included in a nonhierarchical larger "society."[1]
Leopold's reading of Thoreau crept into his schoolboy letters,
and later, during a long convalescence from illness, he read
Thoreau's *Journals*, a wedding gift from his mother (*AL*, 16,
128). He regarded himself as modernizing Thoreau because
Thoreau "wrote before ecology had a name, before the science
of animal behavior had been born, and before the survival of
faunas and floras had become a desperate problem" (*CSCA*,
287). While Thoreau did not know the ecological sciences, he
did anticipate them and was absolutely right, Leopold believed, in understanding that "in wildness is the preservation

of the world." Leopold's account of his own conversion from an anthropocentric to an biocentric perspective in his "Thinking Like a Mountain" essay concludes with a common variant of that Thoreauvian dictum: "in wildness is the salvation of the world" (*SCA*, 133).

Joseph Wood Krutch made his mark on readers by eloquently capturing modernist pessimism in the humanistic conclusions of *The Modern Temper* (1929): "Ours is a lost cause and there is no place for us in the natural universe, but we are not, for all that, sorry to be human. We should rather die as men than live as animals" (169). Later, he overcame that sense of alienation, reversing his perspective and rejoicing in the kinship he felt between humans and all other life. Thoreau's life and work were central to Krutch's conversion. Krutch's biographer believes that Thoreau was responsible for showing Krutch "the way beyond . . . despair"; Thoreau demonstrated that " 'there can be no very black melancholy to him who lives in the midst of Nature and has his senses still.' "[2] Certainly, Krutch's published works prove the centrality of Thoreau's example to his own life. In 1948 he contributed *Henry David Thoreau* to the widely read American Men of Letters series. Following that volume, Krutch published *Great American Nature Writing* (1950), which begins with a long essay identifying Thoreau's central position in the nature-writing genre, followed next by a more specialized essay on "Thoreau and the Thoreauists" (John Muir and John Burroughs). He even published imaginary conversations between Thoreau and Samuel Johnson, Thoreau and George Bernard Shaw, and Thoreau and himself.

Krutch's identification of the important elements of Thoreau's ideas quickly becomes a list of the most important aspects of Krutch's own ideas presented in more than a dozen volumes of writings about nature published before he died in 1970. The most often repeated features are Thoreau's biocentricity (the equality of all living things), close observation of natural fact, emotional participation in the processes of nature, and a scientific bearing that rejected "official science." Thoreau's essays, Krutch says, present the outline of elements defining the modern nature essay which he, himself, learned to compose. The essays combine "scientific knowledge with both philosophical interest and an emotionally charged attitude toward nature."[3] That emotionally charged attitude, at base, says Krutch, comes from a "sense of oneness" with our "fellow creatures." No one before Thoreau, Krutch points out, "had ever taken quite so literally the term 'fellow creatures' " (*GANW*, 5). Radically biocentric, Thoreau

> was tender toward inferior creatures . . . because he did not think of them as inferior; because he had none of that sense of superiority or even separateness which is the inevitable result of any philosophy or any religion which attributes to man a qualitative uniqueness, and therefore inevitably suggests that all other living things exist for him. (*GANW*, 6)

Consonant with Aldo Leopold's argument in *A Sand County Almanac* the same year, Krutch describes Thoreau's biocentric attitude as one that represents "a sort of ultimate democracy which proclaims that all living things, not merely all men, are born with an equal right to life, liberty, and the pursuit of happiness."[4]

Edward Abbey agrees with Krutch in all respects. In a characteristically extreme statement, a nod to Thoreauvian exaggeration, Abbey ventures further than any of the other writers to claim that "even a rock is a being, a thing with character and a kind of spirit, an existence worthy of our love." (*AR*, 128). Abbey justifies such exaggeration with a quotation from Thoreau: "You must speak loud to those who are hard of hearing" (*DR*, 35).

Abbey is concerned with the hard of hearing, those who lead deadened urban lives, who have never experienced a spiritual and political freedom found in wilderness and which the State, big business, and technological progress endanger. In "Down the River with Henry Thoreau," Abbey mingles an account of a rafting trip down the Green River in a wilderness area of southeastern Utah with commentary from and about *Walden*. The Thoreau who compels Abbey is the Thoreau absolutely committed to freedom, whether in wilderness or in the body politic. Thoreau, he writes, becomes more significant with each passing decade. The deeper our United States sinks into industrialism, urbanism, militarism . . . the more poignant, strong, and appealing becomes Thoreau's demand for the right of every man, every woman, every child, every dog, every tree, every snail darter, every lousewort, every living thing, to live its own life in its own way at its own pace in its own square mile of home. (*DR*, 36)

Like Krutch, Abbey admires the Thoreau willing to immerse himself in nature's particulars, rather than the Emersonian side of Thoreau given to mystical abstraction. Abbey admires the Thoreau advocating unofficial science rather than a science that is normally taught in classrooms and practiced in laboratories, divorced from emotion and imagination provoked by recurrent, direct encounters with nature afield. Sounding like Thoreau, Abbey writes that "science in our time is the whore of industry and war" and allies himself with the kind of reason that is "intelligence informed by sympathy, knowledge in the arms of love," the kind of scientific outlook Thoreau and Krutch advocated (*AR*, 125). Above all, it is the independent-minded Thoreau who connects most completely with Abbey's sense of himself, the Thoreau who wrote, " 'If I repent of anything, it is very likely to be my good behavior. What demon possessed me that I behaved so well?' " (*DR*, 23). Abbey, a political anarchist, admires "Civil Disobedience" as much as *Walden* and quotes Thoreau in an epigraph to *The Monkey Wrench Gang* (1975), the novel that inspired the formation and environmental guerrilla tactics of Earth First!: "Now. Or never." Critic Ann Ronald summarizes the two men's common beliefs "in the joys of solitude, in the need for wilderness, in the enormity of big government, and in the efficacy of studied dissent."[5] The title *One Life at a Time, Please*, a volume of Abbey's essays about nature, politics, and writing, suggests his affinity with Thoreau by echoing Thoreau's deathbed comment to a Christian encouraging him to think about the afterlife—"One world at a time."[6]

Annie Dillard's *Pilgrim at Tinker Creek*, while Christian in perspective, is in many ways the work most like *Walden* of any in contemporary American nature literature. Dillard's own description of her first-person, spiritual questing in the natural solitude of rural Virginia makes the connection explicit:

> I propose to keep here what Thoreau called "a meteorological journal of the mind," telling some tales and describing some of the sights of this rather tamed valley, and exploring, in fear and trembling, some of the unmapped dim reaches and unholy fastnesses to which those tales and sights so dizzyingly lead (12).

As Kierkegaard's existentialist phrase "fear and trembling" indicates, Dillard's state of mind is often most like Thoreau's fearful state on Mt. Katahdin (to which she refers) or his disgust when he observed the disheartening sight of a vulture feeding on carrion.[7] Noting the pervasive importance of Thoreau to Dillard, Mary McConahay points out instances in which Dillard "repeats passages from Thoreau . . . and appropriates themes, direction and symbols from her transcendental mentor."[8] Indeed, parallels are numerous between Thoreau's physical and symbolic Walden Pond and Dillard's physical and symbolic Tinker Creek. Beside the water, the two spiritual seekers ritually cleanse themselves so they can awaken and see. "We must learn to reawaken and keep ourselves awake, not by mechanical aids, but by an infinite expectation of the dawn," Thoreau writes; and Dillard echoes and extends the suggestion, encouraging readers "to anticipate, not the sunrise and the dawn merely, but if, possible, Nature herself" (*PTC*, 11).

While nature is symbolic as well as factual for Dillard, she joins Krutch and Abbey in stressing a Thoreauvian emphasis on the empirical rather than Emersonian abstraction alone. The Thoreau who captures her imagination is the one who tells us not to "underrate the value of a fact; it will one day flower in a truth."[9] Playing with language as Thoreau might, she follows a mystical moment in *Pilgrim at Tinker Creek* with the observation that when she sees truly, "as Thoreau says, I return to my senses" (34). The sensual apprehension of natural phenomena is a prerequisite for mystical apprehensions during which she has returned to her senses or, in other words, gotten in touch with reality. That the particular must not be ignored is a central topic of Dillard's book linking natural preoccupations with theological dilemmas. That "Christ's incarnation occurred improbably, ridiculously at such-and-such a time into such-and-such a place, is referred to . . . as 'the scandal of particularity.' Well, the 'scandal of particularity' is the only world that I, in particular, know" (81). Particularity, Dillard argues, whether in the form of improbable religious historicity or horrifying, violent, and ugly natural events, must be accounted for in a comprehensive understanding of God and nature. In the Thoreauvian tradition, Dillard shares with Leopold, Krutch, Abbey, and Snyder what Gary McIlroy characterizes as "a philosophy which seeks truth from facts, meaning from methodology, and coherence overall."[10]

Among these writers, Gary Snyder's connections to Thoreau are most obvious and far reaching. In formative periods of his life, Snyder read and reread *Walden* and essays such as "Civil Disobedience" and "Walking." He studied *Walden* first while a student at Reed College, again while a fire lookout on Sourdough Mountain in 1953, and then again while writing his brilliant poem sequence, *Myths & Texts*.[11] *Myths & Texts* concludes with "The sun is but a morning star," which is also, of course, the last line of *Walden*. Bob Steuding points out that *Walden* and Snyder's work are identical in their religious character, emphasis on the organic and cyclic, reverence for all life forms, and cosmic optimism.

Thoreau provides Snyder with a model for finding the universal in the local. Snyder has become a proponent of the bioregional movement, which identifies Thoreau as its earliest spiritual guide. Resisting mass culture and nationalism, Snyder and other bioregionalists encourage us to learn the prehistory and natural circumstances of our locales. For Snyder, whose own home is in the foothills of California's Sierra Nevada, this means knowing about the native peoples who know how to live harmoniously with nature. Snyder combines the wisdom of native people with Buddhist insights. In this fashion he can step outside the ideologies of contemporary, technologically-driven corporate America and become a voice for wilderness. Like Thoreau, who combined positive attitudes toward Indians and Oriental philosophy and practices, Snyder combines them to champion the spiritual value of wilderness.

Snyder, more than most Americans, lives according to Thoreau's example through his dedication to simple living and spiritual practice, his individualism and self-reliance, a commitment to local community, his principled political stands against materialism and militarism, and his craft as an artist. As poet, Snyder stands squarely in the Romantic tradition, believing that clear vision and precise language bring into correspondence the inner and outer worlds, the private and the public worlds, the wild and the civilized.

Henry David Thoreau's life and writing, then, resonate in the work of the most active twentieth-century Americans who base their writing in the experience of nature. What I have said about Aldo Leopold, Joseph Wood Krutch, Edward Abbey, Annie Dillard, and Gary Snyder applies in varying degrees to other writers who write about personal experiences in nature while raising philosophical, spiritual, and social questions. That company includes, among others, A. R. Ammons, Wendell Berry, John Hay, Barry Lopez, Peter Matthiessen, Michael McClure, Richard Nelson, Terry Tempest Williams, and Ann Zwinger. Each has responded to Thoreau's intuited sense of organic wholeness, which the individual apprehends by paying attention to the near-at-hand, to ants, plants, sunfish, skunks, and stars. All of these writers long for, or actually herald, the affirmation Thoreau records in the "Spring" chapter of *Walden*—that "there is nothing which is not organic" (308). New versions of Romantic organicism and holism inform late-twentieth-century responses to nature.

Thoreau's organicism, of course, did not benefit from the ecological sciences. But his was an ecological view in the making that had its origins in the divided stream of eighteenth-century science. Resisting a mechanistic scientific outlook associated with Francis Bacon, Isaac Newton, Rene Descartes, and Carl Linnaeus that desacralized nature, disconnected emotion from the study of nature, and emphasized human dominion over other forms of life, Thoreau along with other Romantics drew from a counter-tradition. The "arcadian" tradition drew instead from Gilbert White, Henry More, and John Ray and persisted in the works of Henri Bergson and many nineteenth- and twentieth-century writers of the natural history essay. It envisioned nature as organismic, imbued with spirit, knowable through subjective experience in addition to rational thought. It believed that nature's mysteries are best approached with a humility that does not assume that nature exists for human purposes. Donald Worster, historian of the idea of ecology, finds in Thoreau's life and work "an increasingly complex and sophisticated ecological philosophy" growing within the arcadian strain of science that gained more prominence during the Romantic movement (*NE*, 58).

Developing scientific data and scientific conceptions consistent with that "increasingly complex and sophisticated ecological philosophy" became the work of a growing number of biologists, beginning in the late nineteenth century and continuing today. What was originally an intuited, religious belief became scientific truth. Scientists developed concepts and language that describe nature as a whole made up of communities kept stable by a variety of parts in interdependent relationships.

At the turn of the century, pioneer ecologist Henry C. Cowles described the process of "succession" of plants on Lake Michigan dunes by studying more than the individual plants; he described mutual dependencies of plants, the soil, and the climate in a "complex organism."[12] Scotch biologist J. Arthur Thompson used the phrase "web of life" to characterize the special nature of these communal dependencies. In 1915, Liberty Hyde Bailey, a biologist at Cornell University, contributed the term "biocentric" to the vocabulary of ecology, contrasting biocentricity with the anthropocentric, humanistic view that the earth exists solely to meet human needs. In the following two decades, American midwestern ecologists Frederic Clements and Victor Shelford wrote about "biotic communities," or "biome," thus extending the idea of plant succession leading to a stable state of "climax" to include animals. Aldo Leopold's friend Charles Elton, the distinguished professor of zoology at Oxford, contributed to the growing store of ecological conception and imagery by introducing the metaphors of "food chain" and biotic "pyramid"; large numbers of simple organisms formed the base of the pyramid with far fewer large carnivores at the pinnacle, all dependent upon one another through eating and being eaten. The term "ecosystem" appeared in 1935 as Arthur G. Tansley encouraged a less anthropomorphic view than one encouraged by the more popular conception of ecological "community," a word that from the beginning (and for many even now) has been the identifying word for ecology. Tansley and Herbert Gleason, moreover, quarreled with Clements's ideas about succession and climax. Objecting to Clements's idealization of nature unchanged by human contact, they described climax states that are biological systems "artificially created by humans . . . but as stable and balanced as Clements's primeval climax—a permanent agricultural system, for example" (*NE*, 240). A later generation of ecologists, which includes brothers Eugene Odum and Howard T. Odum, who were influential among biologists, social scientists, and humanists alike, has emphasized "energetics," the flow of energy through systems, which for some scientists and many nonscientists is consistent with Romantic holistic, organic thinking.[13] And by mid-twentieth century, Thoreau's ecological philosophy had undergone a modern refurbishing in Alfred North Whitehead's philosophy of science, emerging fully dressed in scientific data, conception, and vocabulary.

Aldo Leopold and Gary Snyder are the most thorough and competent in integrating ecological science with social and philosophical perspectives, articulating, in essence, positive myths or world views that are best described as ecological. Joseph Wood Krutch also turned to biology to support his intuitions about human oneness with nature. Annie Dillard ransacked the works of a wide range of scientists—physicists and chemists as well as biologists—to explore her crisis of spirit. Edward Abbey, the least given to extended commentary upon modern science, nonetheless finds science as the essential touchstone for distinguishing what is true, real, and valuable from what is illusory and wrong.

Throughout his professional life, Aldo Leopold, the only trained scientist in this group of writers, studied ecological principles as they were being formulated, applied them to his field work as a forester and wildlife ecologist, and used them to establish a conservation philosophy that included an ethic for human conduct in relation to the natural environment. His earliest professional articles contain signs that he would eventually become famous for linking the science of ecology with an ethical perspective. In a 1920 article, for example, when ecology was emerging from its infancy, he cited biblical passages that presaged what he would eventually call an "ecological conscience." A passage from Isaiah, Leopold noted, indicates that the prophet had some knowledge of "forest types and the ecological relation of species" as well as "the succession of forest types" (*RMG*, 76). Leopold admired Ezekiel's "doctrine of conservation" in this passage: " 'Seemeth it a small thing unto you to have fed upon the good pasture, but ye must tread down with your feet the residue of your pasture? And to have drunk of the clear waters, but ye must foul the residue with your feet?' " (*RMG*, 74).

As early as 1924 Leopold was applying Frederic Clements's concepts about plant ecology and succession to Arizona brush fields that had been grazed or burned (*RMG*, 114–22). Letters between Leopold and Clements in 1930 about population cycles suggest a wide correspondence between the two men. Further work in ecology grew out of Leopold's friendship with Charles Elton, which began in 1931 at a conference in Canada, continued for many years, and included a visit with their wives at the beloved Wisconsin "shack" that is the real and symbolic center of the "County" in Leopold's *Sand County Almanac*. The association was significant for both: Leopold's biographer writes that "Elton was laying the foundations of ecology; Leopold was attempting to apply the science even before its foundations were set" (*AL*, 284). It was a union of the theorist and the field man. Eventually, Leopold would so distinguish himself as a field ecologist and as the first professor of wildlife ecology at the University of Wisconsin that he was elected president of the Ecological Society of America.

Gary Snyder has had no formal training as an ecologist; nonetheless, he has thoroughly integrated ecological conceptions into his understanding of nature's operations, as well as his social, spiritual, and aesthetic perspectives. From his earliest works, such as the essays in *Earth House Hold* (the title refers to the literal meaning of ecology) to the later collections of poems, *Axe Handles* (1983) and *Left Out in the Rain* (1986), he has drawn upon the writings of such distinguished ecologists as the Odum brothers and Ramon Margalef. For them, and for Snyder, nature's organic unity is most clearly seen in the flow of energy through ecological systems, through "networks" and "loops." For Snyder, scientific information and concepts about natural communities are helpful in establishing better human communities. The "food chain," "succession," "climax," "biomass," "feedback loops," "recycling," and other ecological commonplaces are crucial metaphors for Snyder, pointing the direction for overcoming social and spiritual dislocations. Snyder has steeped himself in ecological thought because, as he says, "far-out scientific knowledge and the poetic imagination are related forces," and because the "ecological sciences are laying out (implicitly) a spiritual dimension" (*OW*, 63).

Joseph Wood Krutch found in Aldo Leopold his example of the man with Romantic ideas that many "would dismiss as 'sentimental' " but which are the ideas of a " 'practical' scientific man" (*VD*, 193). Krutch's most important essay on conservation, in fact, frankly acknowledges his indebtedness to Leopold's seminal essay, "The Land Ethic." In "Conservation Is Not Enough," Krutch writes, "Every day the science of ecology is making clearer the factual aspect" of the "moral law" that "unless we share this terrestrial globe with creatures other than ourselves, we shall not be able to live on it for long" (*VD*, 195). If humans are to live "healthily and successfully," we must, he concludes, "acknowledge some sort of oneness" with the natural "community" that ecological science describes as having "remote interdependencies which, no matter how remote they are, are crucial even for us" (*VD*, 194, 195).

For Krutch, that sense of "some sort of oneness" was the cardinal experience in nature that he sought to validate rationally and scientifically. That basis for a sense of unity and kinship, he determined, was shared consciousness between humans and other life forms. In short, he turned to science to examine the Romantic concern with consciousness. While modern natural and social sciences had, for the most part, banished this topic as irrelevant, Krutch argued that the reality of the subjective life is what we are most certain of, and he turned for support to a great Harvard biologist, William Morton

Wheeler (1865–1937). A pioneer in the study of social insects, particularly ant communities, Wheeler wrote many articulate essays for an educated lay audience describing features of ecological communities and, more specifically, arguing that the Darwinian principle of natural selection was inadequate for explaining evolution. Krutch found in Wheeler's essays congenial arguments for seeing evolution as a drama in which consciousness emerged throughout nature. Subsequently, the subjective life accounts for the most puzzling and interesting insect, bird, and animal behavior. A Romantic preoccupation with consciousness, Krutch determined, was perfectly consistent with contemporary biology and ecology.

Like Thoreau, Annie Dillard faced the problem of "how to reconcile the sometimes oppressive weight of scientific discovery with the broader intuitions of the soul."[14] Neither her reading in modern biology nor her nature essays emphasize the ecological; instead, they evoke the popular Darwinian imagery of gratuitous waste, grotesque violence, and an endless round of propagation and death. Nonetheless, she longs for a reconciliation between mind and spirit, science and religion. The book that had the most impact on her knowledge of natural activity Dillard describes as "a small blue-bound book printed in fine type on thin paper like The Book of Common Prayer"— Morgan's *Field Book of Ponds and Streams*.[15] Like the other biological books Dillard refers to, it is not ecological, and the phenomena she often observes are anything but evocations of benign interdependency.

For Annie Dillard, the emergence of twentieth-century physics—especially Heisenberg's Uncertainty Principle, which acknowledges that absolute scientific objectivity is impossible—permits reaffirmation of a Romantic vision.[16] Physicists Werner Heisenberg, Sir Arthur Eddington, and Sir James Jeans point the way beyond determinist, mechanistic causality. But even her allusions to biologists who describe a savage nature— especially Henri Fabre and Edwin Way Teale, both of whom portray an insect world that seems "the brainchild of a deranged manic-depressive with unlimited capital"—reveal Dillard's Romantic hope that empirically honest attention to natural phenomena will somehow lead to spiritual rest (*PTC*, 67).

Fabre and Teale are at least as well known for their cosmic optimism and expressions of kinship with nature as for their por-
trayals of a violent insect world.

Nor does Edward Abbey turn to the details of ecological information and concept as have Aldo Leopold, Gary Snyder,
and Joseph Wood Krutch. Neither does he allude frequently to
the range of scientists and scientific works that dot the pages of
Annie Dillard's essays. Nonetheless, science is central to his
world view. "Democritus, Galileo, Copernicus, Kepler, Newton, Lyell, Darwin, and Einstein," Abbey writes, are "liberators
of the human consciousness," because they have expanded
knowledge and awareness more than "all the pronouncements
of all the shamans, gurus, seers, and mystics of the earth, East
and West, combined" (*AR*, 125). He stakes out a position identical to the Romantic position found in Leopold, Krutch, Dillard, and Snyder: science is necessary, but it is not sufficient.
One needs to train the rational mind through study of scientific
concepts allied to direct experience with natural phenomena,
but one must also discipline the intuitive faculties through aesthetic practice and openness to mystery. The landscape of the
Colorado Plateau, for example, can best be understood by

> poets who have their feet planted in concrete—concrete data—
> and by scientists whose heads and hearts have not lost the capac-
> ity for wonder. Any good poet, in our age at least, must begin
> with the scientific view of the world; and any scientist worth lis-
> tening to must be something of a poet, must possess the ability to
> communicate to the rest of us his sense of love and wonder at
> what his work discovers. (*JH*, 87)

Like Thoreau, Leopold, and Krutch, Abbey rejects "official science" which is content with the knowable.

The allusions Abbey makes to science are not to ecologists,
distinguishing him from Leopold, Snyder, and Krutch. The Romantic emphases upon cooperation, interdependency, and
mutuality, which found congenial counterparts in ecological
concepts and language, coalesce in a slightly different manner
for Abbey, but they nevertheless unite biology with cooperation rather than with savage struggle. Abbey encountered such

a union in his study of anarchist theorist Pyotr Kropotkin (1842–1921), wrote a master's thesis on anarchism, and maintained a lifelong involvement with anarchist thought. Kropotkin's most important and widely read book, *Mutual Aid* (1902), made a profound impression on Abbey, as it did on Gary Snyder. Kropotkin, a biologist as well as anarchist revolutionary, argued that evolution occurs not because of violent competition but because of cooperation. *Mutual Aid* presents that argument as a description of nature's activities and then applies the same principles to the evolution of societies. Abbey's novels and essays demonstrate repeatedly that he advocates Kropotkin's anarchist political views, and occasionally they show that he accepted his biological views as well. For instance, Abbey comments upon the relationship between science and the knowable in an essay, ending a passage about the behavior of buzzards with a droll allusion to Kropotkin's *Mutual Aid*:

> [T]he buzzards keep an eye on one another as well as on the panorama of life and death below, and when one bird descends for an actual or potential lunch its mates notice and come from miles away to join the feast. This is the principle of evolutionary success: mutual aid. (*DR*, 52)

These five kindred spirits—Aldo Leopold, Joseph Wood Krutch, Edward Abbey, Annie Dillard, and Gary Snyder—represent the persistence of Romantic ideas enlivened and informed by new conceptions and information from the biological sciences. And they share other striking elements. They each acknowledge dramatic conversions in their thinking, feeling, and behavior that turned them from modernist alienation characteristic of mainstream American literary intellectuals to affirmations based upon experiences in nature. Aldo Leopold "converted" from managing wildlife to "thinking like a mountain," accepting a place in nature that acknowledges interdependency and accepts mystery; Annie Dillard's accounts of nature's grotesquery as signs of a maniacal God are counterbalanced by mystical experiences such as seeing the ordinary "back yard cedar" transfigured, "each cell buzzing with flame," and feeling "for the first time seen, knocked breathless by a powerful glance" (*PTC*, 35). Even Edward Abbey, who says "to hell with mysticism," finds "antidotes to despair" in acknowledging and embracing "mystery" (*AR*, 90). In wilderness he found "the discovery of the self in its proud sufficience which is not isolation but an irreplaceable part of the mystery of the whole" (*AR*, 88).

These private conversions are freighted with social and political import. While it is commonplace to say that nature writers as a group are apolitical, that idea is misleading. All but Annie Dillard in this group of writers are known as social critics. Leopold, Krutch, Snyder, and Abbey are profoundly committed to a democracy they see threatened by alliances between materialism and uncontrolled technology. Leopold wrote about "diminishing returns in progress" and feared that because of "mechanized man" the land would not survive (*SCA*, xvii, xviii). Similarly Krutch urged Americans to resist social pressures to give up being *"Homo sapiens*, or man the thinker," and to become merely *"Homo faber*, or man the maker" (*MLO*, 325). To a person, they take bold public stances on topics that have become the staples of environmentalism: pollution, overpopulation, the depletion of natural resources, and the steady erosion of wilderness. Abbey's dedication in *The Journey Home* announces his political stance: "for Paul Revere Abbey, my father, who taught me to hate injustice, to defy the powerful, and to speak for the voiceless." Similarly, Gary Snyder assumes it his responsibility to be a voice "in the councils of government" for the voiceless, "for animals, birds, fish, even mountains" (*TI*, 108). Each section of his political broadside "Four Changes," against overpopulation, pollution, and materialism, contains recommendations for political action, including a "massive effort to convince the governments and leaders of the world that the [problems are] severe" (*TI*, 92).

One reason these writers are labeled apolitical is that they are as uncomfortable with mainstream politics as they are with orthodox science or conventional religion. Leopold and Krutch eschewed Republican and Democratic Party affiliations, but they were tireless in speaking before sportsmen's organizations and chamber of commerce groups. Abbey allied himself with the anarchist environmental activism of Earth First! and contributed a foreword entitled "Forward!" to the organization's manual, *Ecodefense: A Field Guide to Monkeywrenching* (1987). Snyder is a major voice for the alternative politics of the Deep Ecology movement and bioregionalism. For Snyder attacks on science and technology are straw men because we need to address the central political question, "Who is being served by them?" (*RW*, 147). Abbey calls science and technology whores of industry and war, and Snyder would agree (*AR*, 125). Furthermore, all these writers are moralists who want to establish a framework of values within which one can make political decisions concerning environmental matters. Their spiritual conversions and stands on public policy are inseparable.

To experience a sense of wholeness that overcomes modernist fragmentation, these writers require aesthetic experience and expression to accompany spiritual and political renewal. For them, experiencing and writing about nature satisfy needs for beauty and mystery. One of Leopold's signal accomplishments was to unite an ecological view and a land ethic with an aesthetic. Leopold's "land aesthetic enables us to mine the hidden riches of the ordinary; it ennobles the commonplace; it brings natural beauty literally home from the hills" (*CSCA*, 168). The sublime as the standard of beauty institutionalized in national parks such as Yosemite is revised and extended to embrace "fallow fields, bogs, and ponds on the back forty" (168). Leopold and Krutch, moreover, embraced as their literary mission to write about the commonplace in such a way as to evoke poetic intensity. For Krutch, the student as well as practitioner of the nature essay, this poetic quality was a defining attribute of the genre. Because of her eye for nature's grotesqueries, one might overlook Annie Dillard's ecstatic experience of beauty in nature, but repeatedly, she is caught by surprise and overwhelmed by the beauty in the ordinary—a mockingbird's seemingly spontaneous and careless dive, feeding sharks illuminated in green waves. "There seems to be," she writes, "such a thing as beauty, a grace wholly gratuitous" (*PTC*, 8). An important theme of *Pilgrim at Tinker Creek* is that nature's beauty is both concealed and revealed, just as God is both hidden and glimpsed. But the hiddenness does not keep her from perceiving, accepting, and loving a nature that includes her and "whose beauty beats and shines not *in* its imperfections but overwhelmingly in spite of them" (248).

Abbey and Snyder, too, express through their art an unqualified joy in the absolute beauty found in nature. In "A Writer's Credo," Abbey says that it is his obligation to "oppose, resist, and sabotage the contemporary drift toward a global technocratic police state," on one hand, and, on the other, "[t]o honor life and to praise the divine beauty of the natural world" (*OL*, 177–78). Sounding for the moment like Annie Dillard, he says that "Sometimes I am appalled by the brutality, the horror of this planetary spawning and scheming and striving and dying," but he comes to realize that "we have . . . the beauty of art and nature and life, and the love which that beauty inspires" (*JH*, 57). Gary Snyder believes that the delight in being alive and responsive to beauty is a joy that is caught as a kind of energy in poems. It is a "renewable energy" whose source is "the delight of being alive" and will "still be our source when coal and oil are long gone" (*TI*, 113–14).

Considered together, these writers have, with varying degrees of self-consciousness, fashioned a mythic view—an integrated world view in which their experience and knowledge of the natural world are consistent with their social and political vision, their spiritual lives, and their aesthetic. In realigning their personal and public lives, as well as their intellectual and artistic practices, they all have overcome the malaise of rootlessness; they have found places where they feel at home. After lamenting in 1929 that the modern world "is one in which the human spirit cannot find a comfortable home," Joseph Wood Krutch went on to find one in the desert Southwest.[17] Traveling to Arizona for the first time, he experienced "a sudden lifting of the heart" and felt "as though I had lived there in some happier previous existence and was coming back home" (*MLO*, 309, 307). Fellow easterner and adopted Arizonian Edward Abbey learned that "my home is the American West. All of it" (*JH*, xiii–xiv). He writes that he was a "displaced person" who "has been looking for a place to take my stand." *The Journey Home: Some Words in Defense of the American West* is "the story of how I discovered my home" (xiv).

Adams' woods on Tinker Creek becomes Annie Dillard's home in the sense that Walden was Thoreau's. She understands that learning who she is, and what kind of a God there is, is partly the story of determining what is occurring in the nature close at hand. Intimate knowledge of the lives of caterpillars, newts, bluegills, turtles, muskrats, starlings, and herons brings her disorienting moments of feeling "lost, dumbstruck," followed by mystical affirmations of being found, as when she feels "for the first time seen," or knowing that Tinker Creek is the answer to Thomas Merton's prayer to "give us time" (6, 104). Creekside is where she grows up, and the book's litany of childhood's pastimes, games, experiences, thoughts, and emotions leads to a concluding prayer of thanksgiving and praise as she walks along the creek (279).

For Aldo Leopold and Gary Snyder, a prerequisite for overcoming displacement is to recover a place's history, both natural and human. On a bus trip through Illinois, Leopold saw farms that had the look of money in the bank but were ecologically impoverished. For the other passengers "Illinois [had] no genesis, no history, no shoals or deeps, no tides of life and death" (*SCA*, 127). The Leopold family "shack" in Wisconsin's "sand county" became his spiritual home. There Leopold attended to the "ticking of the geological clock" and recounted the history of the land's soils and waters, the story of the interplay between land features and the succession of trappers, settlers, and modern inhabitants who drained marshes and remained ignorant about the undomesticated plants and animals about them. With his family, Leopold spent weekends learning about his place and nurturing it back to health, healing its wounds.

In his own recovery of the land's story, Leopold was doing what Gary Snyder advocates for us all—re-inhabiting place. In the "Shasta bioregion" (his name for Northern California) Snyder has created his literal as well as spiritual home. "Home—deeply, spiritually—must be here," and one must know its ecological and anthropological histories (*PW*, 40). Thus, Snyder argues, one recovers the earth's "wisdom" as well as the wisdom of native people. Ultimately, the person re-inhabiting a place comes to learn that "[t]o know the spirit of a place is to realize that you are a part of a part and that the whole is made of parts, each of which is whole" (*PW*, 38).

2
Aldo Leopold: Mythmaker

Animal and vegetable life is too complicated a problem for human
intelligence to solve, and we can never know how wide a circle of
disturbance we produce in the harmonies of nature when we throw
the smallest pebble into the ocean of organic life.
—George Perkins Marsh (1864)

We are still in Eden; the wall that shuts us out of the garden is our
own ignorance and folly.
—Thomas Cole (1835)

Aldo Leopold was born in Burlington, Iowa, in 1877, the year
when two brothers shooting at Muskego Lake, Wisconsin,
"bagged 210 blue-winged teal in one day" and a dozen years
before "the last passenger pigeon collided with a charge of shot
near Babcock" (*SCA*, 15, 13). Leopold would become one of the
century's foremost conservationists and author of the environmental classic *A Sand County Almanac*. Educated at the Yale
School of Forestry, which had been endowed by the Pinchot
family, Leopold joined the United States Forest Service, then
headed by Gifford Pinchot, Teddy Roosevelt's chief forester
and the nation's most prominent conservationist. Under Pinchot, conservation [was] development, the use of the natural
resources now existing on this continent for the benefit of the
people who live here now."[1]

Beginning in 1909, Leopold spent fifteen years in New
Mexico and Arizona managing millions of board feet of timber
and making policy for public land use by cattle and sheep
ranchers. But by 1915 he had become so concerned about game
depletion in the Southwest that he, an avid hunter, shifted
from a preoccupation with forestry toward the protection of
game. As a leader of the fledgling New Mexico game protection

23

movement, he learned more about relations between game depletion and deteriorating habitat. One result of his growing
awareness of environmental degradation was his important
recommendation that a half million acres in Gila National Forest be preserved as roadless wilderness.

In 1924 illness forced him to transfer to a desk job as asso-
ciate director of the Forest Products Laboratory in Madison,
Wisconsin, but four years later he accepted funding from the
Sporting Arms and Ammunition Manufacturers Institute so he
could conduct game surveys in the north central states. Back in
the field, he sharpened earlier insights from his days in the
Southwest and extended them into ideas about managing
game through attention to improving habitats, eventually publishing *Game Management* (1933). The book relied upon new ecological ideas from pioneering studies, such as Charles Elton's
Animal Ecology (1927). Elton, one of Leopold's regular corre-
spondents, argued that "the concept of food chains [is] the basic organizing principle of the community."[2] That concept of
community would become central to Leopold's ideas about
how an ecologically understood nature works, and during the
thirties it would be combined with ideas and images from other
pioneering ecologists, eventually getting its most succinct and
memorable formulation in his essay "The Land Ethic." There,
"community" includes "soils, waters, plants, and animals, or
collectively: the land" which is "not merely soil; it is a fountain
of energy flowing through a circuit of soils, plants, and animals" (*SCA*, 239, 253).[3]

Game Management earned Leopold the title of "Father of
Game Management," and in 1933, its year of publication, the
University of Wisconsin created a department of game management, naming him professor and chairman. Training a new
generation of influential conservationists, Leopold taught there
until his death in 1948 from a heart attack suffered while fight-
ing a brush fire on a neighbor's farm. The following year,
Leopold's family and friends arranged publication of the manuscript of essays he was completing as *A Sand County Almanac
and Sketches Here and There* (*AL*, 224–25). Reissued with additional essays in paperback in 1966 as *A Sand County Almanac:
With Essays on Conservation from Round River*, it became one of

the environmental movement's "holy books," Wallace Stegner observes (*CSCA*, 233), as does Leopold's biographer, Curt Meine, referring to it as the "bible" of the movement (*AL*, 526).

The outline of his career commands respect but does not prepare one for the remarkable place Leopold holds in the loyalties of both academics and nonacademics. To Roderick Nash, the foremost historian of American attitudes toward wilderness, Aldo Leopold is a "prophet," the same accolade used by others as early as 1954 and often thereafter in places as diverse as in a *National Geographic* feature essay and a movie made for a public television special.[4] Even more specifically, he has been called the environmental movement's Isaiah, Moses, and patron saint (*CSCA*, 75). John Tallmadge concludes that

> Leopold presents himself as a prophet, someone with special knowledge, a history of transformative experiences, and a "strange power of speech." Like the Old Testament prophets, Leopold finds truth in the wilderness and comes back to warn a society with little sense of its own spiritual danger. Like the New Testament prophets, he finds no honor in his own country, which certainly does not wish to be changed. Therefore, he resorts to the only weapons prophets have ever been able to wield: the strength of truth and the transforming powers of language. He takes his place with Thoreau as an American Jeremiah, judging his culture against the standard of wild nature. (*CSCA*, 122)

Actually, for thousands in the environmental movement of the 1960s to 1990s, Aldo Leopold is honored in his own country as a prophet who became the spokesperson for an "ecological conscience," saying "a thing is right when it tends to preserve the integrity, stability, and beauty of the biotic community. It is wrong when it tends otherwise" (*SCA*, 262). That conscience identifies values that promise the restoration of "harmony" between the human and other natural communities. If it is not obeyed, he argued, greed and violence against the land lead to Armageddon as surely as military arms races.

The power of Leopold's life and work, particularly the enormous appeal of *A Sand County Almanac*, is the power of the prophetic. A prophet voices a myth through symbolic anecdotes that create a sense of life's wholeness in ways that go beyond logic, thus allowing people to live with contradictions and uncertainties. The prophet tells the truths that are deep within the collective experience. Leopold's own words show that he understood that a prophet is "one who recognizes the birth of an idea in the collective mind, and who defines and clarifies, with his life, its meaning and implications."[5] The aggregate of those ideas is a narrative that orders time morally, explaining the meaning of a group's origins and destiny. It presents the deepest understanding of the relations among the natural, social, and spiritual worlds. A myth distinguishes positive from negative values and presents heroes and villains who embody those values. It provides a sense of coherence and meaning to life, a unity of thought, feeling, and action. That *A Sand County Almanac* has done so is in the testimony of influential living figures who followed Leopold, such as Wendell Berry, Wes Jackson, and Wallace Stegner, as well as in the book's resonances with those who have gone before him, most notably Henry David Thoreau and John Muir.

Leopold's prophetic intent is revealed in the book's foreword: "These essays attempt to weld these three concepts": that "land is a community [which] is the basic concept of ecology"; that "land is to be loved and respected [which] is an extension of ethics" and that "land yields a cultural harvest" (xix). Science, ethics, and aesthetics are to be "welded." Students of his work have recognized that Leopold, unlike many other scientists, did not think of his scientific activity as separate from economics, politics, and philosophy; "[h]e consciously strove for an integrative understanding" (*RMG*, 3–4). *A Sand County Almanac* is a prophetic expression of an American story that attempts to unify elements in conflict—humans and nature, thought and feeling, intention and behavior.

The three-part arrangement of *A Sand County Almanac* is suited to integrative mythmaking. The three sections move from directly experiential essays, whose center is the Leopold weekend retreat "shack" in "Sand County" Wisconsin, to the book's second group of essays, which broadens the subject to Leopold's professional life and the American conservation movement, and then to a final group of essays, whose realm is the mind and spirit and whose focus is philosophical and ethical. The experience of nature is combined with thoughts about nature; personal life is combined with professional life; daily activity is understood and given significance within a framework of ethical and spiritual insight. Peter A. Fritzell notes that Leopold evokes "the American dream of perpetual harmony among self, society, and non-human surroundings." As the book develops, Fritzell continues, "its overt and primary argument moves logically from images of the land community as empirical fact, through the recognition of man's place in land communities, to a plea for ethical standards of land use"; the relation between the three sections "is the relation of percept to generalized observation to concept."[6] Similarly, Sherman Paul has seen a relational mind at work in the book's structure. Each of the three sections presents a different aspect of the author's life: the life amidst the simple rural pleasures during weekends as "the husbandman of wild things"; life in the wild recollected with a sense of loss; and life in the present as a professor struggling with the dilemmas the other sections have raised. The first part recalls the Thoreau of *Walden* in its "participatory seasonal record"; the second evokes Muir's books about the wild and their "double ply of adventure and conservation"; and the third section brings Leopold forward as their successor.[7]

In the aggregate these essays discuss the origins of life in prehuman nature, a time when the tempo of change is marked in evolutionary, geologic time. The annual return of the sandhill crane to the marsh occurs in "evolutionary time" as a "ticking of the geological clock" (*SCA*, 103). The birth and growth of American culture is best recognized through interactions between humans and nature, which proceed at a contemporary tempo set by the machine age, the tempo of "the song of the power shovel" (100). The landscape of modern America in *A Sand County Almanac* consists mainly of worn-out farmland, damaged or "wounded" through ignorance and greed. Prosperous-looking farms mask the impoverishment of the land's variety whereby scientific farming has eliminated "useless" species of flora and fauna. There is cause for sorrow and alarm. Only an ethical and spiritual renewal offers hope for a future harmony among self, society, and nature.

Part I of the book consists of the actual "Sand County Al-

manac." It has an essay for each month of the year, supposedly
written from the vantage of the shack in central Wisconsin, and
establishes Leopold's persona. He contrasts sharply with the
cultural image of the objective scientist in lab coat using formu-
lae understood only by other highly specialized scientists.
Leopold's persona is the field naturalist who has come to science through a child's and sportsmen's love of the out-of-doors.
He is fascinated with, and informed about, natural history in
ways that remove distinctions between professional scientist
and amateur enthusiast. He learns about nature by direct contact with familiar surroundings, equipped as much with wonder, reverence, and appreciation as with classroom learning. A
man of feeling and conviction, he gains our trust as he cham-
pions an unpopular cause (*CSCA*, 131). More elaborately,
Leopold's persona in *Sand County Almanac* is a neighbor-
teacher-prophet who recalls the land's history, describes
present conditions, and speculates about how to act responsi-
bly toward nature. The underlying hope is that nature's
wounds will be healed by a "science of land health" that is,
however, not yet born and actions of an enlightened citizenry
that has not yet been ecologically educated or ethically
equipped (274). If the wounds are healed and citizens educated
and mobilized, Leopold suggests, America's democratic experiment will be revitalized.

Leopold's persona is a twentieth-century variant of the
mythic American yeoman farmer, the traditional repository of
Jeffersonian virtue and homespun wisdom. Leopold's lessons
are drawn from the text of his Wisconsin weekend farm, the beloved shack. In ways familiar to today's bioregionalists,
Leopold "re-inhabited" that place and learned to "dwell" there
in Heidegger's sense of the word.[8] In the November essay, for
instance, Leopold writes, "Every farm woodland, in addition
to yielding lumber, fuel, and posts, should provide its owner a
liberal education. This crop of wisdom never fails, but it is not
always harvested. I here record some of the many lessons I
have learned in my own woods" (78). One woodlot lesson that
is spiritual and aesthetic, as well as ecological, is that all parts of
the ecosystem, in this case diseased trees, have value. With familiar religious allusions Leopold recalls wishing that "Noah,

when he loaded up the Ark, had left the tree diseases behind. But it soon became clear that these same diseases made my woodlot a mighty fortress, unequaled in the whole county" (78). Diseased trees sustain his population of raccoon, ruffed grouse, honeybees, rabbits, chickadees, pileated woodpeckers, wood ducks, and prothonotary warblers. The flash of the warbler's "gold-and-blue plumage amid the dank decay of the June woods is in itself proof that dead trees are transmuted into living animals . . . When you doubt the wisdom of this arrangement, take a look at the prothonotary" (82). This and every essay in the almanac section argue that "every farm is a textbook on animal ecology" and that every farm is a textbook in economics, history, politics, ethics, aesthetics, and matters of the spirit (86). It is a text that, Leopold writes, "enables me, a mere professor, to blossom forth annually as a successful seer and prophet" (77).

This professor-seer-prophet's lectures are not only about nature's workings, according to the ecological sciences, but about historical interactions between nature and society. The persona incorporates the man of civic, as well as private, virtue. While sawing firewood from an oak with eighty growth rings, he comments on the Wisconsin environmental and conservation history which the tree symbolizes. Observing the rings as he cuts through them, he notes major natural events, such as storms, droughts, fires, and insect plagues, while commenting on the history of human destruction of martin, lynx, and passenger pigeons. He talks knowledgeably about changes wrought on the landscape by ignorance, such as farmers' "overwheating" that turned once fertile soil into a sand county and the "progress" that brought steam shovels to suck "dry the marshes of central Wisconsin to make farms, [making] ashheaps instead" (10–16).

Overall, this history of the connections between land and humans is one of loss for both. But not only loss. The year the oak he is sawing was germinated, 1865, was the year John Muir, on a farm like Leopold's, just thirty miles away, offered to buy the land from his brother for a wildflower sanctuary. Thus "1865 still stands in Wisconsin history as the birthyear of mercy for things natural, wild, and free" (17). History, whether in terms of losses or gains, is understood as humans acting within, not outside or above nature. As Sherman Paul states it, Leopold "replaced ego- with eco-thought."[9]

An essential element of "eco-thought" is biocentricity, the view that all life has equal value and that the locus of value is in the biotic community rather than in humans. In part one, Leopold is direct in identifying the "Abrahamic," anthropocentric stance as the source of environmental trouble; in part two, he is direct in portraying his "conversion" to the biocentric position.

The essays in part two, "Sketches Here and Now," emphasize Leopold's life as a professional conservationist who began as a forester, became wildlife manager whose responsibility was to increase populations of game species, but who eventually acquired an ecological perspective. That perspective placed him at odds with conservation bureaucrats and allied him spiritually with Henry David Thoreau and John Muir more than with Gifford Pinchot, Teddy Roosevelt, and Franklin Delano Roosevelt. By 1935 he understood in heart as well as in mind that favoring special economic interests (the lumber industry) and special species (deer) led to local, temporary gains but also to long-term deep losses for human and land communities.

In these essays Leopold announces his separation from turn-of-the-century conservationists' Darwinian view of nature as essentially wasteful. Conservation orthodoxy held that "nature's way of sowing seed is to leave it to the wind, the water, the birds and animals. The greater part falls in a mass close to the parent plant and is shaded out or choked to death by its own abundance." Irrationality and waste are natural; rationality and economy, human. "How different the economy of a rational being!" wrote Lester Ward in 1893. "He prepares the ground, clearing it of its vegetable competitors, then he carefully plants the seeds at proper intervals so that they shall not crowd one another, and after they have sprouted he keeps off their enemies . . . and thus secures . . . the vigorous growth and fruition of every seed planted."[10] This view of the nature-human relationship, Leopold charged, led conservationists to regard "the land as soil, and its function as commodity-production . . . to grow trees like cabbages, with cellulose as the basic forest commodity" (*SCA*, 259).

Such an emphasis on controlling and managing nature meant that engineers and other technical and scientific experts should do the work of conservation; inevitably, they became the heroes of conservation. Leopold, an apostate conservation bureaucrat, developed a low opinion of conservationists' utilitarian ethos and the many government-sponsored activities of the "high priests of progress" (*SCA*, 107). Eventually, he would even look beyond his own ecologically informed profession, "convinced that only ecologically literate and ethically motivated ordinary citizens could effectively conserve privately held, productive land" (*RMG*, 16). In "Marshland Elegy" those well-meaning but ignorant and arrogant, anthropocentric, conservationist "experts" become "villains" who destroy the wild in their single-minded efforts to force nature to serve only human ends. They include engineers, economists, planners, surveyors, CCC road builders, and all the "alphabetical conservationist(s)" in New Deal agencies (107). Elsewhere others are added to the list, for example, farming experts at state colleges, and farmers themselves, who are dedicated to making "Illinois safe for soybeans" (125). Somberly, Leopold asks, "What is a species more or less among engineers? What good is an undrained marsh anyhow?" (107).

But from an ecological, biocentric perspective, "useless" has no meaning. "The last word in ignorance," Leopold writes, is

> the man who says of an animal or plant: "What good is it?" The emerging ecological sciences teach us that if the land mechanism as a whole is good then every part is good, whether we understand it or not. If the biota, in the course of aeons has built something we like but do not understand, then who but a fool would discard seemingly useless parts? (*SCA*, 190)

One Leopold sentence that rephrases Pinchot's belief "that the first principle of conservation is development" highlights the distance between Leopold's biocentric thinking and the anthropocentric thinking of mainstream conservation: "the first principle of conservation" is "to preserve all the parts of the land mechanism" (190).

"Thinking Like a Mountain," the centerpiece essay of the "Sketches Here and There" section, dramatizes Leopold's conversion from the anthropocentric, Pinchotesque strain of conservation to an ecological, biocentric perspective. "Conversion" is not too strong a word, since the essay mythically brings together the objective and subjective, the scientific and the mystical by telling a story of radical change from one world view to another.[11] In this brief, seminal essay, Leopold acknowledges his complicity in "sins" against nature and dramatizes a mystically altered sense of kinship with all things natural.

He recalls the time when he was working in the Southwest and "thought that because fewer wolves meant more deer, that no wolves would mean hunters' paradise" (*SCA*, 138). His view changed "the day I saw a wolf die," watched "a fierce green fire dying in her eyes." He and his companions had spotted a mother wolf and her pups at play, and, following normal western practice, jumped to their feet and began firing their rifles until the pups scattered and the mother lay dying. "I realized then," he continues, "that there was something new to me in [the mother wolf's] eyes—something known only to her and to the mountain" (138). In pedestrian terms, he had learned the ecological lesson that if wolves are killed, deer will increase beyond the carrying capacity of the ecosystem and will destroy the foliage that supports them. The scientific lesson is perfectly consistent with his other, mystical understanding that the "hidden meaning in the howl of the wolf" may be "Thoreau's dictum: in wildness is the salvation of the world," with which Leopold concludes the essay (141).

"Thinking Like a Mountain" is a mythic tale that takes place across two overlapping landscapes. One is mystical and moral; the other is the landscape of scientific study and rational analysis. Leopold fuses the two through his structuring of narrative and use of metaphor. Neither negates the other. Idea and feeling are brought together, as are thought and religious sensibility. Spiritual impulse is as much a part of his professional change from game manager to preservationist as his scientific knowledge. Through plot structure and the simile of "thinking like a mountain," he adopts simultaneously scientific and mystical interpretations of watching the wolf die, making them compatible and inseparable. John Tallmadge concludes that "the narrator's conversion experience . . . [has] turned him into a prophet, thus fulfilling the role he assumed in the foreword," and that the essay's "moral . . . is that everything we thought we understood—the wolf, game management, the raising of livestock, our laws, our politics, even the words of our prophets—must now be reviewed from an ecological perspective" (*CSCA*, 126–27).

As with others who are profoundly interested in nature and in nature-human connections, Leopold's religious feeling is unorthodox. His biographer, Curt Meine, writes that "the intuitive sense of a living earth had always been a part of Leopold's psyche" (*AL*, 214). The Russian mystic Piotr Ouspensky, disciple of the better known George Ivanovitch Gurdjieff, furnished Leopold with intellectual justification for that intuition in *Tertium Organum*, which argued for the compatibility of science and mysticism, before augmenting it with the organicism of ecologists Frederic Clements and Charles Elton (*AL*, 214). Throughout his life, from childhood in a nominally Lutheran household and throughout his marriage to the devoutly Roman Catholic Estella, Leopold was skeptical about organized religion. One of the few times he "consented to enter a church" was for his daughter's wedding (*AL*, 418). Orthodox religion, he noted, had not led people to "any real respect for the one thing in the Universe that is worth most to Mankind— namely Life."[12] Perhaps thinking of his own childhood, Leopold wrote that a boy who was converted from atheism by observing the beauty of warblers and knowing that science could not adequately account for the mysteries of warbler migration had convictions more profound than the convictions of "many inductive theologians" (*SCA*, 230–31). Leopold didn't believe in a personal God. He believed, his daughter concluded, in a "mystical supreme power than guided the Universe . . . akin to the laws of nature." His son Luna concluded that "he, like many of the rest of us, was kind of pantheistic" (*AL*, 506). His religious feeling was closer to that caught in Joseph Wood Krutch's phrase, "we are all in this together,"[13] and to Albert Schweitzer's "reverence for life" with which Rachel Carson so identified that she dedicated *Silent Spring* to him.

Conversion to "thinking like a mountain," that is, respond-
ing to nature holistically, ecologically, and biocentrically, prepares Leopold to espouse a "land ethic" in Part 3 entitled "The
Upshot," of *A Sand County Almanac*. Such an ethic is needed,
Leopold argues, because "philosophy and religion have not
heard of [conservation]" (246). Nor had they heard of the ecological sciences. "The Land Ethic" essay mythically combines
philosophy, religion, science, and political ideology. It offers
hope for an alternative to the ongoing destruction of nature and
deterioration of the quality of life. The essay is Leopold's best
known, most influential, and most mythic.

Superficially, his argument is simple. The essay's eight sections present an ecological account of nature as a "land pyramid" with soil as its base and carnivores at its apex, united
through the intricate interdependencies of food chains, the
"living channels which conduct energy upward" (253). The stability of this "highly organized structure" comes from evolution's tendency "to elaborate and diversify the biota" (253).[14]
Secondly, in addition to lessons in ecological science, there is
the fundamental historical premise introduced in the "January" essay of section one but developed throughout *A Sand
County Almanac* that human and natural history are
interdependent—land conditions influence the course of human history and, conversely, human activity alters the biota.
Thirdly, the ethical proposition is that guides for human conduct are inadequate since people have rights and power while
nature is passive. What passes for a "land ethic" is derived
from laissez-faire economics, which views land as private property to be used as owners see fit. Although the obligation to
protect the land is relegated to governmental agencies, the job
is "too large, too complex, or too widely dispersed to be per-
formed by government" (251).

Facing the dilemma of what ethical guide there can be for
human and nature interactions, Leopold prophesies that we
are approaching a time when we will extend rights to all "citizens" of the biotic community. His hope is based upon a historical pattern he discerns of a continuing expansion of ethical
perspectives and rights concomitant with an expansion of a
sense of community. What once was accepted as property—

Odysseus's slave-girls whom he hanged, for instance—is no longer property. The Ten Commandments were for individuals; later the Golden Rule concerned relations between individual and society (238). The direction is toward increased "modes of co-operation," and the premise of all ethics is that "the individual is a member of a community of interdependent parts" (239). By extension, we will learn to think about the human-nature relationship as other than economic; "the land ethic simply enlarges the boundaries of the community to include soils, waters, plants, and animals, or collectively: the land" (239). Thereby, land acquires rights and people acquire responsibilities.

Thinking about land not as property but as a community of citizens to whom we should (and will) extend rights is, of course, a radical viewpoint. That it has appealed to a wide audience of environmentally concerned people is a testimony to the essay's imaginative and emotional impact as much as its intellectual power. Rhetorically, Leopold manages to clothe his argument in language that blurs distinctions between scientific, social, and spiritual realms, thus appealing to his audience's longed-for reconciliation between science, social conduct, and spiritual belief.

From the beginning of the essay, the argumentation is persuasive as well as logical. The opening argument, for example, intermingles scientific concepts, a historical overview of changes of Western ethical views, religious prophecy, and classical literature. As Donald Worster, the intellectual historian of ecology, comments, one element of Leopold's persuasive strategy is that he appeals to "the perennial hope . . . that science will show the way" (*NE*, 336). Leopold calls upon language of Darwinian science that his audience does accept—ideas about instinct and evolution—to support his radical view. Historical changes in ethics are "actually a process in ecological evolution [whose] sequences may be described in ecological as well as in philosophical terms. An ethic, ecologically," he explains, "is a limitation on freedom of action in the struggle for existence." The ethic has its "origin in the tendency of interdependent individuals or groups to evolve modes of co-operation," which the "ecologist calls . . . symbioses" (*SCA*, 238). Just as an animal's instincts guide its responses to new and complex ecological situations, a land ethic is "a kind of community instinct in-the-making" for knowing how to act in a natural community that is bewilderingly intricate (239). Extending rights to the biota, therefore, becomes "an evolutionary possibility and an ecological necessity" (239). In short, evolutionary mechanisms that created the natural world we understand through the basic principles of Darwinian biology and ecology have an analogue in the development of human ethical systems. Natural and social are analogous; therefore, science is a guide to conduct.

Leopold's rhetoric of persuasion is not only scientific; it is the familiar rhetoric of democratic possibility. The most important word in the essay is "community." The land ethic "simply enlarges the boundaries of the community" to include nature. "Community" for ecologists of Leopold's generation was synonymous with ecosystem, and that "land" is a community of interrelated, interdependent organisms is still, for the lay person, the central insight of the ecological sciences. Clearly, "community" is an anthropomorphic word freighted with associations identifiable with the human experience. If we agree that both society and nature are communities, we are disposed to think of proper ethical relations between human and natural communities as a model for those between nations: peaceful rather than warlike, based upon mutual respect rather than exploitation, characterized by cooperation rather than conflict, by tolerance rather than hatred.

For a Depression and war-weary generation emerging from World War II's defeat of fascism and, later, to a generation longing for relief from Cold War tensions, the utopian rhetoric of community, freedom, inalienable rights, tolerance, and peace that Leopold uses to prophesy his ecological vision was, and is, more than scientific. The war against nature had left the ecologically educated person "alone in a world of wounds" (*SCA*, 272). Ecology and history merge in his imagination as Leopold writes that conquerors are self-defeating because they do not understand "what makes the community clock tick, and just what and who is valuable, and what and who is worthless, in community life" (240). Analogously, "mechanized man" is self-defeating because the biotic community "is so complex that

its workings may never be fully understood" and because economic standards for determining what is valuable and what is
worthless in community life are deficient. The land ethic, he
concludes, "changes the role of *Homo sapiens* from conqueror of
the land-community to plain member and citizen of it" (240).

Integrating heart and mind, the essentials of Leopold's ecological language resonate with two centuries of American democratic idealism. He announces, as Donald Worster writes, a
"Declaration of Interdependence" (*NE*, 333). All living organisms and even the soils and waters become "citizens" who
have "rights"; nature's mysterious equation of diversity with
stability is analogous to the central paradox in democracy—
e pluribus unum. In brief, ecological language fits with the life
experiences of Leopold's New Deal and wartime generation.
Members of that generation were angry about authoritarian violence and frightened by ruthless competition. The rhetoric of
the land ethic invoked reassuring American democratic veri-
ties. The same feelings and ideas appeal to the imaginations of
Americans in later generations who have their own reasons to
fear irrational, authoritarian violence and to hope for peaceful,
democratic lives.

If one message of Leopold's language is that science and a
democratic ethic are compatible with each other, another is that
both are compatible with the essentials of a secularized Judeo-
Christian tradition. What Leopold hoped for, writes Wallace
Stegner, was "the gradual spread of a 'land ethic,' built upon
scientific understanding of the earth and earth processes, but
infused with a personal, almost religious respect for life and for
the earth that generates and supports it" (*CSCA*, 234). The essay's overt allusions to biblical tradition are to Abraham, Ezekiel, and Isaiah. By allusions to Abraham, on the one hand, and
Ezekiel and Isaiah on the other, Leopold identifies a central ambiguity in Judeo-Christian formulations of relations between
humans and nature. "Abraham knew exactly what the land
was for," he writes. "It was to drip milk and honey into Abraham's mouth" (*SCA*, 240). This "Abrahamic concept of land"
Leopold identifies in his foreword to *A Sand County Almanac* as
the egocentric, anthropocentric obstacle to enlightened conservation (xviii). But "Ezekiel and Isaiah have asserted that the de-

spoliation of land is not only inexpedient but wrong" (239). In an essay written in 1939 but not published until forty years later, parts of which were incorporated into "The Land Ethic," Leopold quotes a passage from Ezekiel he might well have been thinking of when alluding to Ezekiel in "The Land Ethic": "Seemeth it a small thing unto you to have fed upon good pasture, but ye must tread down with your feet the residue of your pasture? And to have drunk of the clear waters, but ye must foul the residue with your feet?"[15]

With allusions to Abraham and Ezekiel set in opposition, Leopold reveals a still debated ambiguity in the Judeo-Christian tradition. Since the 1970s, most readers of "The Land Ethic" either have read or have heard versions of Lynn White, Jr.'s argument in "The Historical Roots of Our Ecological Crisis."[16] White argues that the Judeo-Christian tradition and modern science have been anthropocentric. Leopold anticipated White's views, noting that the Judeo-Christian tradition is "premised squarely on the assumption that man is the end and purpose of creation, and that not only the dead earth, but all creatures thereon, exist solely for his use."[17] White, like Leopold, acknowledges a more muted counter tradition—St. Francis of Assisi is his Ezekiel.

Leopold's religious allusions add the weight of the spiritual to scientific-social support for an environmental ethic. The major ethical visions in the Bible, he says, come not from God directly, nor do they originate with prophets like Moses. "Only the most superficial student of history supposes that Moses 'wrote' the Decalogue," Leopold asserts; "it evolved in the minds of a thinking community, and Moses wrote a tentative summary of it for a 'seminar' " (*SCA*, 263). Parallels between Moses' thinking community and Leopold's audience of ecologically informed and democratic citizens, between Moses as prophet and Leopold as prophet writing a summary of a new ethic for a "seminar," are unmistakable. In addition, a number of the values derived from Leopold's understanding of the nature-human relationship coincide with a Christian ethic. Imbedded in the essay's rhetorical strategy is a call to spiritual reformation and to personal responsibility. Prerequisites to right conduct are purification of the spirit by acknowledging the

"sins" of ignorance and greed (ignorance of the "land mechanism" and abuse of economic self-interest) and contemplating
the essentially good and mysterious natural creation that inspires awe, respect, humility, and love.

Finally, more muted than Leopold's integration of scientific, political, and religious rhetoric with the moral is language
that appeals to a longing for physical security, health, and well-
being. Both in this essay and in the essays in sections one and
two of *A Sand County Almanac*, Leopold identifies land with human bodies that may suffer disease but that, with proper treat-
ment, may also return to health. In his "Wilderness" essay, he
makes explicit that body and medicine are analogous to land
and conservation: "There are two organisms whose processes
of self-renewal have been subjected to human interference and
control. One of these is man himself (medicine and public
health). The other is land (agriculture and conservation)" (272).
Organicist ecological thinking had implicitly encouraged a
body/land identification. David Oates writes that when "Aldo
Leopold referred to the 'health' of the land, he was employing
less metaphor than one might think. Ecologists tended to mean
it literally, up to and beyond the time of *A Sand County Almanac*:
the land, the ecosystem, could be literally regarded as a single,
complex, living creature."[18] Leopold was, we know, concerned
with the "health of the forest as an organism" (*SCA*, 196). On
adventures to the Mexican Sierra Madres, he had the insight
that "all my life I had seen only sick land."[19] "The land is sick,"
he writes again in "Wilderness," but mainstream conservation,
"the art of land doctoring," is being practiced vigorously before
a "science of land health [has been] born" (*SCA*, 274). In "The
Land Ethic," he defines "health" as the "capacity of the land
for self-renewal" and "ecological conservation" as "our effort
to understand and preserve this capacity." The individual, acting within the framework of a land ethic, according to an ecological conscience, should take "responsibility for the health of
the land" (258). The individual farmer, Leopold writes in "A Biotic View of Land," should, for example, "include wild plants
and animals with tame ones as expressions of fertility," thereby
contributing to the diversity and stability of the biota, the capacity of the land for self-renewal (*RMG*, 272). In the foreword

to *A Sand County Almanac*, Leopold had warned that our society is "sick" and, by implication, may not return to health until the land is healthy: "Our bigger-and-better society is now like a hypochondriac, so obsessed with its own economic health as to have lost the capacity to remain healthy" (xix). That the renewal of the land's health will be a renewal of the nation's health is Leopold's prophetic message.

In "The Land Ethic," then, Leopold is at his best and most complete as mythmaker. The prophet-professor brings into alignment Americans' deepest political and religious impulses so that he creates a sense of wholeness in our physical, social, and spiritual experience. Our feelings about connections with something greater than ourselves receive scientific justification; distinctions between human and nonhuman communities fade; and the proper guide to conduct in nature is the familiar golden rule of doing unto others what one wishes done unto one's self. More fully, since a major function of myth is to "contain" paradoxes, Leopold's essay, as does the complete *Sand County Almanac*, creates a sense of unity and wholeness that goes beyond unresolved intellectual tensions. There are unresolved tensions—in fact, "The Land Ethic" has as its subject the unresolved tension between self-interest and communal needs. Similarly, an ecological ethic does not resolve tensions between contradictory views about stability and change, between nature as fragile, sick and dying and nature as vigorous, healthy and permanent, or between humans as decent and significant and humans as hateful and insignificant.[20] Nonetheless, in Aldo Leopold's work the coincidence of scientific, moral, religious, and political rhetoric and the larger views that rhetoric denotes and connotes provide a sense of underlying unity. Leopold's mythic perspective in "The Land Ethic," with its powerful combination of language and logic appealing to the audience's sense of universal values, offers encouragement to go on living actively without being paralyzed by those paradoxes. "The Land Ethic," Wallace Stegner reminds us, is a call to action; Leopold's "land ethic is not a fact but a task" (*CSCA*, 245).

"The Land Ethic," then, convinces partially through logic but primarily as an exemplar of homespun American wisdom.

But for a myth to be vital it must be consistent with the best thinking of the times. The question remains, therefore, whether philosophers can take seriously Leopold's argument for a "land ethic."

Some philosophers and historians studying environmentalism, past and present, object to popular enthusiasm for a land ethic. One of the most important objections is that a land ethic based upon ecology's description of nature is a variant of discredited natural law theory which holds that the guide for morality is nature's operations. Most contemporary philosophers and scientists are reluctant to suggest that scientists discover Eternal Law that humans are ethically bound to obey. Philosophically, the problem is the classic Is/Ought dilemma in ethics: are intrinsic values necessarily instrumental values? Those who answer in the affirmative are taking a position Barry Commoner calls a "law" of ecology—"Nature knows best." It is unquestionably the conception behind Aldo Leopold's central moral tenet that "a thing is right when it tends to preserve the integrity, stability, and beauty of the biotic community. It is wrong when it tends otherwise" (*SCA*, 262).

A second, related objection is that the source of moral conviction for land ethic advocates is neither nature nor reason but a vague and antiscientific mysticism. Stephen R. Fox, a contemporary historian of the American conservation movement, acknowledges that "traced back to its ideological roots, conservation amounted to a religious protest against modernity."[21] Lewis Mumford had argued that overcoming modernity requires "something like a spontaneous religious conversion: One that will replace the mechanical world picture with an organic world picture."[22] Aldo Leopold's narrative in "Thinking Like a Mountain" is such a conversion narrative. Other elements that mark Leopold as one among many in the history of environmental concern attracted to religious mysticism include his early fascination with Ouspensky's mystical organicism and, more generally, his prophetic rhetorical stance in the service of the insight that humans and nature constitute a "whole."

John Passmore, the earliest important critic of the logic behind the land ethic, is disgusted with what he regards as such uncritical sentimentality. In *Man's Responsibility for Nature* (1974) he argues in favor of remaining loyal to the humanistic tradition, which, he finds, offers ample reasons for conserving and protecting nature. He identifies his position with rationality, and he identifies mystical dimensions of environmentalism with superstition, charging that "ecologically based protest . . . is being deployed as a new and powerful weapon in the old battle between rationality and mysticism."[23] An ideological debate between Passmore and Leopold would be, no doubt, a variant of the clashes between Gifford Pinchot and John Muir at the beginning of the century.

If Passmore set the agenda for philosophical objections to the logic of a land ethic, philosopher Holmes Rolston III set the agenda for advocacy. Rolston's "Is There an Ecological Ethic?" is, in effect, a defense of Aldo Leopold's basic position and a clear, if provisional, answer to objections from Passmore, Petulla, and others. Rolston addresses the crucial Is/Ought problem that arises from the concurrences between ecological vocabulary and vocabulary that is social, political, aesthetic, and ethical. After identifying parallels between descriptive and value-laden vocabulary, Rolston argues that the " 'ought' is not so much *derived* from an 'is' as discovered simultaneously with it." He continues:

> As we progress from descriptions of fauna and flora, of cycles and pyramids, of stability and dynamism, on to intricacy, planetary opulence and interdependence, to unity and harmony with opposition in counterpoint and synthesis, arriving at length at beauty and goodness, it is difficult to say where the natural facts leave off and where the natural values appear. For some observers at least, the sharp is/ought dichotomy is gone; the values seem to be there as soon as the facts are fully in, and both alike are properties of the system.[24]

Don E. Marietta, Jr., clarifies and extends Rolston's discussion with philosophical and psychological arguments that, he says, explain this "fusion" of fact and values. Marietta's position is

similar to those held by other twentieth-century philosophers
(and scientists) who

> reject the notion that facts are perceived in bare objectivity . . .
> while values are only products of our subject judgment. . . . Such
> a notion of brute, theory-free facts is an obsolete concept. . . .
> Both factual and valuational observations of the world are consti-
> tuted together by consciousness. . . . It is rather a matter of rec-
> ognizing the values embedded in our observations of the world,
> observations in which factual cognition and value cognition are
> fused, only to be separated by reflection.[25]

Eugene C. Hargrove adds a historical dimension to
Rolston's and Marietta's argument about the fusion of fact and
value. In "The Historical Foundations of American Environmental Attitudes," Hargrove reviews Passmore's and Rolston's
antithetical positions and then describes a three-hundred-year
history of the aesthetic values shared between the culture at
large and early botanists, biologists, and geologists. Essentially, Hargrove finds the natural sciences compatible with romantic values, particularly "complexity, diversity, variety, in-
dividuality, and geologic time."[26]

More broadly, both philosopher Baird Callicott and historian Roderick Nash have presented convincing evidence that
the need to widen a humanistic ethic to include rights for the
nonhuman was argued long before Leopold's essay appeared.
Callicott finds preparation for Leopold's claim of an evolving
ethic in Darwin's writings, especially Darwin's turning to "a minority tradition of modern philosophy for a moral psychology
consistent with and useful to a general evolutionary account of
ethical phenomena" (*CSCA*, 190). From that tradition, Darwin
developed a moral view that emphasized feelings in animals,
particularly "parental and filial affections" and "social senti-
ments" (190–91). Furthermore, Darwin knew, anthropological
studies of ethics reveal that "the boundaries of the moral community are generally coextensive with the perceived boundaries of society," and that definitions of "society" and "community" can expand (192). Darwin noted that "social instincts

and sympathies" are at first confined to the family and tribe but expanded to larger communities. Callicott quotes Darwin as saying "there is only an artificial barrier to prevent [man's] sympathies extending to the men of all nations and races" (193). As Roderick Nash points out, Leopold's statement that "the tendency of interdependent individuals or societies to evolve modes of cooperation" known as ethics "nearly plagiarized Darwin" (*RN*, 68). Nash identifies many writers who anticipated Leopold's basic view that we should include nature in our ethical thinking even if they did not have the support of ecological science, for example, William Lecky, Henry Salt, Edward Evans, J. Howard Moore, Liberty Hyde Bailey, and Albert Schweitzer (68).

One need not, then, turn to mysticism and against science to defend a land ethic. To Rolston, Marietta, Hargrove, Callicott, Nash, among others, Leopold's philosophical position in "The Land Ethic" is not antirational mysticism, nor is it outside Western intellectual traditions.

Since the 1970s, when critical attention focused on the position Leopold announced twenty years earlier, differences over the rational merits of Leopold's land ethic have produced a substantial body of books, scholarly articles, and popular journalism. Furthermore, Leopold's advocacy of an ecological conscience has found a central place in tenets of major environmental organizations in a spectrum ranging from the Sierra Club and the National Wildlife Federation on one end to Greenpeace and Earth First! on the other.[27] Debate and advocacy will continue because the essential dilemmas Aldo Leopold articulated in *A Sand County Almanac* have not been resolved. We have not yet, for example, determined where to place the line between responsible use of nature, "intelligent tinkering" as Leopold phrased it, and preservation of a nature that is not fully understood. While there are many instances of ecological perspectives influencing legislation and public policy, the ideological tensions that surface in contests between the rights of private ownership and the public good are rarely eased. The view of land as commodity is still as powerful as the view of land as community.

It was Aldo Leopold's genius that he could synthesize his

outdoor experiences from his boyhood afield in Iowa to family life with his wife and children at their weekend shack in central Wisconsin with a professional life that stirred his imagination as well as intellect about Americans' relations with the land. As mythmaker, he articulated a vision that went beyond a description of nature's workings to offer the possibility of politically and spiritually satisfying lives. In *A Sand County Almanac* and his other essays, he has written about the relations between humans and the rest of nature in ways that have appealed to a deep, intuited sense of what is true and right. For him, and for many who continue to admire his life and work, an ecological, scientific view of nature offers a way to understand the past and to hope for a better future grounded in Judeo-Christian and democratic ideals.

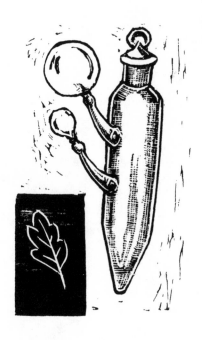

3
Joseph Wood Krutch: Metabiologist

If we are led to believe that what takes place in our mind is something not substantially or fundamentally different from the basic phenomenon of life itself, and if we are led then to the feeling that there is not this kind of gap which is impossible to overcome between mankind on the one hand and all the other living beings—not only animals, but also plants—on the other, then perhaps we will reach more wisdom, let us say, than we think we are capable of.
—Claude Lévi-Strauss (1978)

One thing I'd like to know most of all: when those ants have made the Hill, and all are there, touching and exchanging, and the whole mass begins to behave like a single huge creature, and *thinks*, what on earth is that thought?
—Lewis Thomas (1974)

Only a year after the publication of Aldo Leopold's *Sand County Almanac*, Joseph Wood Krutch opened his *Great American Nature Writing* (1950) anthology with a lengthy epigraph from the beginning of Leopold's book:

There are some who can live without wild things, and some who cannot . . . [W]ild things were taken for granted until progress began to do away with them. Now we face the question whether a still higher "standard of living" is worth its cost in things natural, wild, and free. For us of the minority the opportunity to see geese is more important than television, and the chance to find a pasqueflower is a right as inalienable as free speech.

These wild things, I admit, had little human value until mechanization assured us a good breakfast, and until science disclosed the drama of where they come from and how they live. The whole conflict thus boils down to a question of degree. We of

46

the minority see a law of diminishing returns in progress; our op-
ponents do not. (*SCA*, xvii; *GANW*, n.p.)

Five years later Krutch himself had become a nationally recognized champion of conservation and an eloquent nature essayist. *The Voice of the Desert* (1955), *The Great Chain of Life* (1956),
Grand Canyon (1958), and *The Forgotten Peninsula: A Naturalist in
Baja California* (1961) popularized Leopold's ideas and contributed to a national interest in conservation that was beginning to
remind commentators of the intense interest during the Teddy
Roosevelt era. Bookstores today have still in print no fewer
than eight titles of the more than a dozen nature volumes
Krutch published between his first, *The Twelve Seasons* (1949),
and last, published the year before his death, *The Best Nature
Writing of Joseph Wood Krutch* (1969). Readers have bought more
than 200,000 copies of his nature books celebrating the joy of a
"sense of identity, material as well as spiritual, with [our] fellow creatures."[1]
   Joy is the antithesis of the profound pessimism for which
Krutch was first known. Once, when he was on lecture tour, a
woman approached and asked if he were Mr. Krutch. When he
assured her he was, she responded, "But you do not look as,
as—*depressed* as I expected!" (*MLO*, 211). For her he was the
Columbia University professor of English and drama critic for
The Nation who spoke for his educated generation in 1929 when
he concluded in *The Modern Temper* that "the universe revealed
by science, especially the sciences of biology and psychology, is
one in which the human spirit cannot find a comfortable home
. . . a universe alien to the deepest needs of [our] nature" (xi).
Intellectually, he had always sided with science. Even as a child
in a middle-class family in Knoxville, Tennessee, at the turn of
the century, he recalled, "I took my stand with science against
religion." When he learned of Darwinism, it confirmed his belief that if the lion ever lies down with the lamb "he will starve
to death" (*MLO*, 20). At twelve, he read part of Herbert Spencer's *Synthetic Philosophy* and spent his teenage years as a "devout Spencerian" (22). After graduate study in New York City
at Columbia University, he returned to Tennessee briefly to
cover the Scopes "Monkey Trial" in Dayton as a reporter for

The Nation, siding, of course, with liberalism allied with science against religious fundamentalism. Soon, however, the great nineteenth-century scientific revolutions associated with Darwin, Marx, and Freud had left him estranged from other people and from nature. The best Krutch could do in 1929 for other intellectuals was to counsel stoicism, saying, "We should rather die as men than live as animals"—humans and nature were tragically irreconcilable."[2]

Two decades later, however, in the late 1940s, a transfigured Joseph Wood Krutch listened to the backyard chorus of "Spring Peepers" at Eastertime in Connecticut and expressed the central perception of all those who have cared about nature and have transcended alienation: "we are all in this together." Krutch was experiencing a conversion from modernist alienation to joyful pantheism parallel with Aldo Leopold's conversion from an anthropocentric to a biocentric perspective, which he dramatized in "Thinking Like a Mountain." Variations on this sort of conversion experience, in fact, are recounted by almost every writer who establishes what Emerson called "an original relation to the universe," for example, Annie Dillard's vision of the backyard cedar in flames in the "Seeing" chapter of *Pilgrim at Tinker Creek* and Gary Snyder's profoundly altering insight that everything is alive and that the "life" of a stone is as beautiful and valuable as a human life.

The elements that led to and reinforced Krutch's conversion are easily identified in his writings. In the early forties he became preoccupied with Thoreau and in 1948 published an influential critical biography. For Krutch, Thoreau was a "link between Gilbert White," the great English nature writer, and "more recent writers such as Burroughs and Muir" who "combine, as Thoreau himself would have liked to combine, scientific knowledge with both philosophical interest and an emotionally charged attitude toward nature."[3] His lengthy and thoughtful "Prologue" to *Great American Nature Writing*, written in the late forties, confirms that he had identified a congenial literary and intellectual tradition that countered the Cartesian dualism he held responsible for the cleavage between subject and object, humans and the rest of nature. The Cartesian conclusion "that all the animals except man are mere machines without feeling and without consciousness" is counter-balanced, he asserted, by the conclusions of Thoreau, John Muir, John Burroughs, Edwin Way Teale, Mary Austin, William Beebe, and William Morton Wheeler, among others (16). They invite us to

> [t]ake [our] place in nature and rejoice that it is one vast fellow-ship; that man now has his being, not in the center of a vast ma-chine, but simply as a member of a society every other member of which is, like him, alive, sentient, and capable to some extent of participating in experiences like his own. (26)

Krutch's conversion was completed when he changed landscapes from suburban Connecticut and urban New York to the desert landscape around Tucson, Arizona. The physical re-location mirrored in his daily life the transformation taking place in his intellectual and emotional lives. On his first trip across the desert in 1937 he had experienced "a sudden lifting of the heart" (*MLO*, 308). Feeling like Adam, he said it seemed "as though I had lived there in some happier previous exist-ence and was coming back home" (309, 307). During his second sabbatical year in Arizona (1950–1951), he wrote *The Desert Year* collection of essays recounting why he came to the desert, how he went about seeing it, and what he saw in a year's time; he knew then that he and his wife, Marcelle, "would make a rad-ical break with our past life" (*MLO*, 311).

The Voice of the Desert (1955), among his finest books, shows Krutch's indebtedness to Aldo Leopold and his frank champi-onship of Leopold's vision. Most of the essays focus on features of desert life—the saguaro cactus, roadrunner, scorpion (the first air-breathing creature), a mouse—that raise issues con-cerning ecology, evolution, and conservation-preservation. The genial, informed narrator takes opportunities to pass along information from ecologists—for example, the desert has no "wet or dry season below six feet"—and to draw larger lessons—for example, "In the long run our boasted control of nature is a delusion" (14, 132). Like *A Sand County Almanac*, the book concludes with essays that are broadly social and philo-sophical. The concluding two essays, "Conservation Is Not

Enough" and "The Mystique of the Desert," in fact, are explicit in their indebtedness to Leopold, in their advocacy of a land ethic, and in encouraging readers to speculate beyond biological "collections of observable facts" in attempting to draw moral and aesthetic conclusions (210).

For Krutch, Leopold was the model for such advocacy and speculation. Leopold, Krutch writes, argued that conservation based upon "enlightened selfishness" does not work. Citing "The Land Ethic" (and even its original version in the *Journal of Forestry*), Krutch paraphrases Leopold's argument that humans must extend toward nature "love, some feeling for, as well as some understanding of, the inclusive community of rocks and soils, plants and animals, of which we are a part" (*VD*, 193). "Every day," Krutch writes, "the science of ecology is making clearer the factual aspect" of "a moral law" that "unless we share this terrestrial globe with creatures other than ourselves, we shall not be able to live on it for long." Ecology teaches this by identifying "more and more remote interdependencies which . . . are crucial even for us" (195). While Leopold's position ordinarily might be dismissed as "sentimental," Krutch recommends it as that of a " 'practical' scientific man" (193).

After quoting Thoreau that "the world which we inhabit is more wonderful than it is convenient; more beautiful than it is useful; it is more to be admired than it is to be used," Krutch quotes further from Leopold's argument that conservation will not succeed through more conservation as usual but only through " 'an ethical relation to land' " involving " 'love, respect and admiration for land, and a high regard for its value. By value, I of course mean something far broader than mere economic value; I mean value in the philosophical sense' " (*VD*, 200). In "The Mystique of the Desert," a companion essay to "Conservation Is Not Enough," Krutch praises Leopold for surpassing science, technology, and traditional conservation to make "metabiological" recommendations that fuse science, ethics, and aesthetics (212–13).

Grand Canyon: Today and All Its Yesterdays shows that Krutch, always the intellectual, had absorbed Leopold's perspective in *A Sand County Almanac* and was grounding himself in the history of American thinking about nature. The books' essays frequently allude to early American writer-travelers like William Bartram, explorers of the Southwest canyon country such as John Wesley Powell, political figures like Teddy Roosevelt, and ecologists ranging from Ernst Haeckel, who coined the term "ecology," to pioneering ecologist C. Hart Merriam, who in the 1890s devised the theory of ecological "zones," to contemporaries like Aldo Leopold (118, 122–23). His extended portrait of the Grand Canyon emerges within the historical framework of American thought about nature, especially as recently influenced by the ecological sciences. He encourages the canyon's visitor to understand that "whatever aspect of the changing scene he may take note of, it is part of a larger picture in which geology, climate, vegetation and animal life are all linked together. The forests are there because of the mountains and the jays because of the pines" (122).

Clearly, Joseph Wood Krutch's "conversion" from rational man who perceived alienation as the logical consequence of scientific knowledge, especially in the biological and psychological sciences, to pantheist and nature advocate did not lead him to reject science. As a responsible voice for conservation and environmentalism, he could not ignore or reject the science he had held responsible for the alienation of modern intellectuals. To do so in any case was not his inclination, as can be seen in his wide reading and in his attraction to Aldo Leopold, a "man of science." But another scientist, himself a popular writer, was more important than all the others in showing Krutch how to be scientifically responsible while at the same time joyously affirming a mystical "oneness" with all of nature. That scientist was Harvard entomologist William Morton Wheeler (1865–1937).

Wheeler's biological work and metabiological speculations lent scientific authority to Krutch's intuition that all living creatures are linked. More specifically, Krutch, like Wheeler, argued that consciousness, the subjective life, is the source of kinship feelings between humans and animals. Joseph Wood Krutch found what was for him a scientifically justifiable rationale for affirming a mystical insight that humans were not, finally, alienated from the creation around them. Nature essays were Krutch's medium for uniting his direct experience of nature, scientific information, metabiological discussion, and the expression of deep feeling.

Krutch, of course, was not trained in science, nor would he ever claim expert biological knowledge. Instead, he was the amateur scientist, the naturalist who went afield as much for aesthetic delight and spiritual nourishment as for scientific knowledge. He was, nevertheless, one of those amateurs afield whom Leopold and other scientists defended as important to nature study. Wheeler, too, eloquently defended the amateur scientist; and Wheeler's essays became Krutch's guide for incorporating science into a new, enlarged, and positive frame of reference.

Krutch's biographers have left unmentioned Wheeler's influence, perhaps because Wheeler died ten years before Krutch began writing nature essays and there was no correspondence between the men. But Krutch's references to Wheeler are frequent and important. Wheeler, moreover, was one of his generations's outstanding biologists. His more famous Harvard colleague, Alfred North Whitehead, said that Wheeler was the only man he had ever known "who would have been both worthy and able to sustain conversation with Aristotle."[4] Until his death in 1937, Wheeler was a brilliant researcher in insect social behavior who also wrote masterful popular essays about the philosophical implications of modern biology. One of these essays includes a passage to which Krutch often alluded and which evokes the wonder of our kinship with the living world while also suggesting the limits of scientific methods and knowledge:

> Why animals and plants are as they are, we shall never know, of how they have come to what they are, our knowledge will always be extremely fragmentary because we are dealing only with the recent phases of an immense and complicated history, most of the records of which are lost beyond all chance of recovery, but that organisms are as they are, that apart from the members of our own species, they are our only companions in an infinite and unsympathetic waste of electrons, planets, nebulae and suns, is a perennial joy and consolation.[5]

Krutch had found a scientific authority who not only was modest about the powers of science, but, more importantly, was able to express a deep kinship with the living world despite the threat of meaninglessness that modern science presented.

An authority on ant communities and the social behavior of ants, Wheeler was fascinated with parallels between nonhuman and human life. Resisting mechanistic and reductionist colleagues, just as Eugene and Howard T. Odum would for postwar ecologists, Wheeler was drawn to speculative topics that engaged psychologists and philosophers more often than biologists. And he did so in the name of biology:

> I have acquired the conviction that our biological theories must remain inadequate so long as we confine ourselves to the study of the cells . . . and leave the psychologists, sociologists, and metaphysicians to deal with the more complex organisms. Indeed our failure to cooperate with these investigators in the study of animal and plant societies has blinded us to many aspects of the cellular and personal activities with which we are constantly dealing. This failure, moreover, is largely responsible for our fear of the psychological and metaphysical, a fear which becomes more ludicrous from the fact that even our so-called "exact" sciences smell to heaven with the rankest kind of materialist metaphysics. (*EPB*, 7)

Biology was necessary for understanding nature, of course, but it was not enough. One had to be a "metabiologist," the term Krutch had borrowed from George Bernard Shaw to apply to Leopold. The metabiologist believes, as did Wheeler and Krutch, "that life is not completely explainable in merely physical terms" and that psychological, philosophical, "moral and aesthetic questions should be discussed in connection with what we know about living creatures" (*VD*, 209).

For Wheeler and Krutch, the limitations of Darwin's mechanism of natural selection was the perfect example of this dictum. For mechanistic biologists in early Darwinian debates, and for their behaviorist descendants, the principle of natural selection abolished the necessity to discuss purpose, will, consciousness, and intelligence in accounting for evolution. But Wheeler and Krutch did believe that discussions of psychological agencies, especially human and animal consciousness, were relevant to understanding evolutionary processes. Wheeler's biographers point out that his biological specialty disposed him to resist the growing number of scientists who accepted the central role of random mutations in natural selection: "Working with ants and other social insects as he was, [Wheeler] simply found it difficult to believe that random mutations were capable of creating all the exceedingly complex and highly adaptive behavior patterns of these insects."[6] Wheeler argued bluntly that modern biological study left an organism so "inexplicable" that, in addition to biology, "we should do better to resort to psychological agencies like consciousness and the will" (EPB, 25).

Mechanists irritated Wheeler, but so did those who claimed metaphysical agencies at work beyond or through evolution. He dismissed all metaphysical entities, such as fellow entomologist Henri Fabre's deity, Henri Bergson's "elan vital," or Hans Driesch's vitalist conception "entelechy." Wheeler came to a conclusion that emphasized, as did his argument against the mechanists, the place of psychology in biological thought: "Even the subconscious and the superconscious [sic] are more serviceable as explanations than such anemic metaphysical abstractions" employed by Fabre, Bergson, Driesch and others (25).

A summary of one nature essay in The Voice of the Desert, the often anthologized "Moth and the Candle," can illustrate how deeply Wheeler's views influenced Krutch. The essay blends scientific information with metabiological speculation based upon the limits of biological and religious explanations:

Alone at night in the Arizona desert, Krutch observes a moth and its symbiotic relationship to a yucca plant seed pod called a "candle," and in passing shows that he has done his scientific homework by referring to the studies of "the remarkable . . . entomologist Charles V. Riley" (82).

Krutch sees and records behaviors that positivistic science cannot account for and which are not to be found in scientific journals. Centrally, the moth goes through "a series of purposeful actions"; we find ourselves, Krutch writes, "compelled to say that it 'knows what it is doing' " (82).

Krutch continues by acknowledging that finding purposeful activity in nature is Darwinian heresy, which lays him open to the charge of vitalism, but he asserts that he does accept the Darwinian version of evolution as "overwhelmingly clear" (87). One exception, however, is that uncritical reliance upon the role of "minute, accidental variation and natural selection" leaves too many unsolved mysteries (87). Metabiological speculation is permissible, because it is not entirely clear how evolution occurs.

These mysteries would be diminished, Krutch argues tentatively but persistently, "if only we might assume the intrusion of some factor not wholly accidental and mechanical." If only we could assume "some intelligence, however feeble; some intention, however dim; some power of choice, however weak, which the evolving organism could have used to take advantage of the opportunities which chance provided" (88).

Doing his charming best to anticipate and disarm the critics who will charge him with sentimentality, amateurism, and vitalism, Krutch concludes with a summary of three basic positions, all involving inherent difficulties in attempts to explain the behavior of the moth with the candle: the mechanistic, which most biologists would accept but Krutch would not; the equally unacceptable religious position that, he points out, entomologist Henri Fabre would offer; and the one, he says, "few are willing to admit" but which, to him, is "not wholly improbable," that purposeful activity of some kind operates in "lower" forms of life (97).

The parallels and identities between Krutch's ideas in "The Moth and the Candle" and Wheeler's ideas and information are unmistakable: both men object to the dominant role of accidental variations in accounting for evolutionary change and, consequently, to mechanistic reductionism; and both resist theological explanations of deity at work either outside or within nature.

It is equally unmistakable in "The Moth and the Candle," and in many of Krutch's other essays, that both men are preoccupied with the role of the subjective life in evolution and with their realization that a subjective life in humans and nonhumans is at the heart of the kinship humans feel with living nature. We are all in this together because we share consciousness with other creatures.

According to Wheeler, the major problem with the mechanists' position, which descends from "Descartes's interpretation of animals as creaking machines," is that it presents twentieth-century biologists with "grave difficulties" when attempting to account for the "genesis of intelligence and consciousness" that they either have "ignored, minimized, slurred over, or produced by some kind of prestidigitation from conflicting unconscious instincts or reflexes" (*EPB*, 45–46). An acknowledgement of the subjective life, consciousness, in humans and animals was Wheeler's answer to religionists and vitalists, too, since as already noted he preferred psychological entities to metaphysical agencies such as Fabre's God and Driesch's entelechy. In the same vein, Krutch boldly states, "What the mechanist disparagingly calls 'the *subjective*' is not that of which we are least, but rather that of which we are *most* certain."[7] The certainty of the subjective life is his answer as well to advocates of religious positions that rely upon the existence of a soul: "Whereas the soul is difficult to define, much less to demonstrate, 'consciousness' is self-evident."[8] The "feeble intelligence" Krutch asked readers to consider as contributing to behavior in "The Moth and the Candle" is an echo of one of Wheeler's central tenets—that a

> feeble intelligence could conceivably build up in the course of ages a considerable and complicated fabric of instincts and structures, a fabric so impressive that in all plants and in many animals we might be unable to detect the diminutive intelligence by which it had been so slowly and painfully initiated and elaborated. (*EPB*, 50)

Both men believed that theories of "emergent evolution" could account for some kind of intelligence throughout living nature. Wheeler had written a book on the subject, as well as an essay that appears in the popular *Essays in Philosophical Biology*, and Krutch comments similarly in his essay "The Stubborn Fact of Consciousness." Such theories posit that in the course of evolution, intelligence appeared and became a new "factor capable of originating changes of its own."[9] These theories of emergent evolution were commonplace in the 1920s, one of

Wheeler's most professionally active decades. Their content varied from large claims the theologically inclined often made, to the most modest claims, such as those Wheeler advanced. Not unlike Pierre Teilhard de Chardin in our own times, the more influential emergent evolutionists of the twenties, such as Lloyd Morgan, Jan Smuts, and Samuel Alexander, saw progression from the emergence of time-space, to matter, to life, to mind, and finally to a spirit that legitimizes faith in deity. Wheeler, however, could not tolerate the "ghostly presences" he found in the theories of Morgan, Alexander, and others. Wheeler stayed closer to the process of natural selection and the emergence of mind for his explanations, concluding that "even the lowest organisms have a glimmer of intelligence" (*EPB*, 150, 50).

Krutch's most extended incorporation of emergent evolutionist ideas into his essays occurs in *The Great Chain of Life*; there, like Wheeler, he uses emergent evolution to account for the appearance of consciousness in general and intelligence in particular throughout the animal world. One intention of the book, Krutch says in an aside, is "to suggest in as many different ways as possible that to call man 'an animal' is to endow him with a heritage so rich that his potentialities seem hardly less than when he was called the son of God" (153–54). In the Prologue he raises the question of whether man is like a god, a machine, or an animal and then chooses, of course, the last (vii). The essays that follow highlight identities between human and "lower" forms of life. Salamanders have "some sort of awareness" that insects don't have and humans do have in greater measure, squirrels have the capacity to amuse themselves with playful activity, birds express joy, and bighorn sheep courage (144). Throughout nature Krutch finds signs of awareness, of joy and love, and of intelligence. We are discovering, he speculates, that animals "exhibit, in rudimentary form, some of the very characteristics and capacities whose existence in ourselves we had come to doubt because we had convinced ourselves that they did not exist in the creatures we assumed to be our ancestors" (143). Each essay in *The Great Chain of Life*, in effect, unfolds more completely the basic contentions of "The Moth and the Candle." Krutch often speculates that questions that can't be answered by appealing to natural selection can be resolved "if we are willing to accept the possibility that what nature has been working toward is not merely survival; that, ultimately, it is not survival itself but Consciousness and Intelligence *themselves*—partly at least for their own sake" (122).

Krutch knew that his views opened him to charges of anthropomorphism. His arguments, in fact, are classically anthropomorphic. Wheeler's own cautiously sympathetic description of the anthropomorphic view of instinct can be used to summarize Krutch's approach: "It is essentially a recognition of the fundamental identity of animal and human souls, the differences between which are regarded merely as differences of degree of development. This implies that intelligence is not exclusively human." (*EPB*, 47). Krutch's strategy was simply to acknowledge the charge and deflect it by noting that "the risk of attributing too much" to plants and animals seems "no greater than the risk of attributing too little."[10] Wheeler's strategy for deflecting the same charges was similarly more rhetorical than analytical. Wheeler says the term *anthropomorphism* was rightly used in theological controversies, but involved mere mudslinging in biological debates. Since man is an animal himself, he writes, man can interpret other animals only in terms of himself. The charge of anthropomorphism "can only mean that he continually runs the risk of attributing to animals a greater development of intelligence than they possess," but scientific methods and experiment rectify this tendency so that "it is impossible to regard anthropomorphism as a very terrible eighth mortal sin" (*EPB*, 46). Essentially, Krutch and Wheeler both admitted sinning, but did so in a way that reminded their audiences of the limitations of behaviorism, making their transgression seem minor. They glossed over the issue.

Most contemporary biologists, consequently, would dismiss their views as unworthy of serious consideration. An important exception is animal behaviorist Donald R. Griffin, professor of biology at Rockefeller University, past chair of Harvard University's biology department, the preeminent student of animal consciousness, and the foremost writer of scholarly and popular articles and books on the subject.[11] Like

Wheeler and Krutch, he has been drawn to metabiology, to speculation about what can not be authoritatively answered through
conventional scientific activity. In what he calls his "prescientific"
studies (which we can call metabiological) Griffin analyzes "several of the more significant new developments in ethology,
psychology, and neurobiology from a cognitive point of
view."[12] As recently as 1992 in *Animal Minds*, Griffin elaborated
extensively upon an insight stated fifteen years earlier that
Wheeler and Krutch would find acceptable and supportive:

> It may be helpful . . . to assume some limited degree of conscious
> awareness in animals, rather than postulating cumbersome
> chains of interacting reflexes and internal states of motivation.
> Behavior patterns that are adaptive in the evolutionary biologist's
> sense may be reinforcing in the psychologist's terms, as well.
> Perhaps natural selection has also favored the mental experiences
> accompanying adaptive behavior.[13]

Griffin includes an instructive response to the charge of anthropomorphism that is leveled against anyone who speaks of
"animal consciousness." He writes that "it is actually no more
anthropomorphic, strictly speaking, to postulate mental experiences in another species than to compare its bony structure,
nervous system, or antibodies with our own." The problem has
been that we have had no "effective methods for detecting
[mental experiences] reliably in other species, let alone analyz-
ing them by scientific methods."[14] But Griffin goes on to stand
behaviorist objections on their heads by presenting the hypothesis that:

> as mental experiences are directly linked to neurophysiological
> processes—or absolutely identical with them according to strict
> behaviorists—our best evidence by which to compare them
> across species stems from comparative neurophysiology. To the
> extent that basic properties of neuron, synapses, and neuroendo-
> crine mechanisms are similar, we might find comparably similar
> mental experiences.[15]

Griffin would agree with Krutch that the "stubborn fact of
consciousness" in human and other life should not be ignored

just because modern biological sciences are not ready to study it on a large scale or because critics dismiss as anthropomorphic informed speculation about bonds between the human and the nonhuman. Here, Griffin's position becomes identical with Wheeler's and Krutch's: the intellectual risk of attributing too many human qualities to animals is less than the risk of attributing too few.

Krutch's metabiological speculations about a shared consciousness between humans and nonhumans, based upon his ruminations about biology and psychology, the sciences he had singled out in 1929 as the most alienating, led him to metaphysics of a sort. In this he went beyond his guide, William Morton Wheeler. While Wheeler had flirted with vitalism, particularly Henri Bergson's, he eventually distanced himself from such views. Krutch occasionally criticized vitalism, but a vitalist undercurrent in his work is revealed in admiring allusions not only to Bergson and George Bernard Shaw but to others, including geneticist Edmund Ware Sinnott, one of the few vitalists contemporary with Krutch.[16] In the 1950s vitalism was no longer a responsible position for most intellectuals, but Krutch was not willing to put vitalist arguments completely aside.

While mystical writers were foreign to Krutch in their clarity of vision and certainty of conviction, his intense experience of joyful kinship with nature led to moments when he felt "no longer a separate selfish individual but a part of the welfare and joy of the whole" (*VD*, 215). He learned that "the acute awareness of a natural phenomenon . . . of the living world is the thing most likely to open the door to that joy we cannot analyze" (215–16). It is an experience universal among nature writers, even the most skeptical. For instance, Edward Abbey, himself a religious skeptic, recounts in "Coda: Cape Solitude" a time when, alone, he stared into the abyss of the Little Colorado River gorge and understood that despair could be replaced by self-forgetful joy: "The despair that haunts the background of our lives . . . can still be modulated . . . into a comfortable melancholia and from there to defiance, delight, a roaring affirmation of our existence. Even, at times, into a quiet and blessedly self-forgetful peace, a modest joy" (*AR*, 195). While Krutch was usually self-conscious about revealing his mysticism and awkward in expressing it, his mystical response to nature is evident in the joyful phrase from his first nature essay that "we are all in this together."[17] In his best works Krutch was not so self-conscious about his mystical impulses and occasionally discussed them directly. For instance, commenting about what he had attempted in *The Voice of the Desert*, he wrote in 1954 that the reason for his "deepest caring" is beyond the scope of "biology or even metabiology" and that it is found only by "admitting the mystical element" (214). Just before his death in 1970, Krutch tried to state the source and nature of his faith, which was, as for many nature advocates, homemade:

> It is a faith in nature as creative force . . . It is even, if you like, a religion. It puts your trust not in human intelligence but in whatever it is that created human intelligence and is in the long run, more likely than we to solve our problems. . . . If God did not create Nature, then perhaps Nature is creating God.[18]

In his earliest writings about nature, Krutch called his perspective "pantheism." The term implies, he wrote, "that life itself rather than something still more mysterious called the 'cause of life' is the bond between fellow creatures" (*GANW*, 73). Considering that Aldo Leopold's organicism was drawn from Ouspensky and his religious position, according to his son and daughter, was pantheistic, Krutch could have made Leopold his example. But for his example of a pantheism that recognized material as well as Thoreauvian spiritual bonds between humans and other life-forms, Krutch turned for the best statement of this "feeling for nature" to "a writer who was first and foremost a great scientific observer"—William Morton Wheeler (*GANW*, 73).

In essay after essay, whether in his nature essays or in the kind of social and philosophical commentary that won a National Book Award for *The Measure of Man: On Freedom, Human Values, Survival and the Modern Temper* (1954), Krutch brought into focus the relationships among science, human values, the bond between humans and other life-forms based upon sharing various qualities, and the particulars of his own experience in society and nature. That combination of elements defined for Krutch the essential elements of the nature essay. He had placed himself squarely in the tradition he had outlined in *Great American Nature Writing*.

Peter Fritzell acknowledges Krutch's Prologue to *Great American Nature Writing* as "the first notable attempt by an established literary critic to declare nature writing a distinct genre and to account for its history" (41). The Prologue presents "the essential critical and historiographic terms—the underlying categorical distinctions and the view of history—that . . . still control the discussion of nature writing as a literary form" (41). While Fritzell laments that Krutch did not have the benefit of "the years of structuralism, deconstructionism, and their aftermaths" for understanding "the literary history and criticism of nature writing," he can offer no better example of someone understanding "the interplay in nature writing among the forms of impersonal science, autobiography, and philosophy" (86). Certainly, in practice, Krutch was true to his own view that the best nature writing brings together personal experience in nature, information and ideas that are scientific (but not necessarily sanctioned by "official science"), positive emotions of "fellow feeling" with all life, and metabiological speculations that are philosophical, aesthetic, and spiritual.

Various conclusions may, of course, be drawn from Krutch's odyssey from alienated twentieth-century intellectual to joyful postwar pantheist and nature writer. One conclusion, surely, is that metabiological speculation based upon his experiences in nature and reading in "humanistic evolutionists" like Aldo Leopold and William Morton Wheeler allowed him to reverse the bleak outlook of *The Modern Temper* and affirm that metabiology allows us to see that the universe partially revealed by science, especially the sciences of biology and psychology, is one in which the human spirit can find a comfortable home, a universe responsive to our deepest needs. That Krutch's formal thinking and casual musings turned so frequently upon scientific topics and resulted in more than a dozen widely read books published primarily in the 1950s indicates that he and his readers found science the necessary touchstone for certifying authoritative truths that buttressed their larger world views, their myths. In his essays readers could find responses to their spiritual longing, their need for a reconciliation with nature, and an accommodation with society. These essays' pervasive ethical, social, and aesthetic themes were rooted in personal experience on one hand and abstract biological science on the other. Ambivalent about science and opposed to "scientism," Krutch and Leopold, as would Gary Snyder in the next generation, appealed to those like themselves, who longed nevertheless for scientific verification of positive beliefs by finding within mid-twentieth-century biology a counter-tradition to alienating science.

Krutch's use of Wheeler, Leopold, and others in his nature essays furthered a long-standing academic and popular examination of the relations between science and broader cultural matters. Many would agree that the positivistic tradition, which included the mechanists and utilitarians who were the targets of Leopold's and Wheeler's barbs, has been the authoritative scientific tradition. But a counter-tradition with adherents among scientists as well as laypersons has supported Leopold's and Krutch's romantic values. Historian of biology Peter J. Bowler points out that works of evolutionary humanists such as Julian Huxley's *Evolution in Action* (1953) and George Gaylord Simpson's *The Meaning of Evolution* (1949), for example, "were intended explicitly to go beyond the technical details of the theory into broader vision of the nature and purpose of life. . . . Both writers strove to get away from the mechanistic image of science by stressing the creative, opportunistic aspects of life's development within the Darwinian scheme."[19]

Joseph Wood Krutch contributed to the popular nature essay tradition by writing its history and, at the same time, by writing some of the most enjoyable and interesting essays in that tradition. He not only became one of the most widely read Americans in the decade of the fifties who advanced Aldo Leopold's land ethic as a basis for a new conservation, but he contributed to the ongoing American discussion about the relations among science, nature, and human values. His union with nature restored to him a sense of personal wonder about the myriad forms of life around him. His phrase that "we are all

in this together" signifies that, on the one hand, he apprehended that union mystically; on the other hand, he made the
connection intellectually through his reading of metabiological
works. Joseph Wood Krutch's nature essays demonstrate that
his curiosity about links in feelings and thoughts between humans and other animals was unceasing and that the kinship he
found as a result brought him a sustaining joy.

4
Edward Abbey:
An "Earthiest"

I love Nature partly because she is not man, but a retreat from him.
None of his institutions control or pervade her. There a different kind
of right prevails. In her midst I can be glad with an entire gladness
—Henry David Thoreau (1853)

I admit to mystery / in the obvious
—A. R. Ammons (1974)

In the last formal interview Joseph Wood Krutch granted, fellow transplanted easterner and now fellow Arizonian Edward
Abbey asked him whether cars should be banned from all national parks. Allowing that Yellowstone Park might be a lost
cause, Krutch said that he could see no need for roads in the
new Canyonlands National Park. "[T]oo many people use their
automobiles not as a means to get to the parks but rather use
the parks as a place to take their automobiles," Krutch com-
mented (*OL*, 184–85), sounding much the same as his interviewer, who in *Desert Solitaire*, published almost simultaneously with the interview, inveighed against "Industrial
Tourism" (*DS*, 45). The national parks slogan, "Parks are for
people," Abbey wrote in his polemic, should be decoded as
"parks are for people-in-automobiles" (50). "What our national
parks and forests really need," Krutch added, "are not more
good roads but more bad roads. . . . There's nothing like a
good bad dirt road to screen out the faintly interested" (*OL*,
185). Characteristically, Abbey would go farther, stating the
first of his several "sensible proposals" for saving "both parks
and people": "No more cars in national parks" (*DS*, 52).

Edward Abbey admired Krutch for his "unwavering insistence . . . on the primacy of freedom, purpose, will, play, and joy, and on the kinship of the human with all forms of life" (192). He shared in some of Krutch's essential metabiological speculations, as in the following passage from *Desert Solitaire*. To Abbey, the "singing" of frogs after a desert rain seems as much an expression of "spontaneous love and joy" as of territoriality: "Has joy any survival value in the operations of evolution? I suspect that it does; I suspect that the morose and fearful are doomed to quick extinction. Where there is no joy there can be no courage; and without courage all other virtues are useless" (125).

He could not have been more congruent with Krutch in his thinking about joy as a survival mechanism. But the range and depth of Abbey's affirmations, especially his spiritual resiliency, have not always been apparent to his readers. One reason is that the playfulness and humor that pervade his work, setting him apart from others who write about nature and accounting for his wide popularity, divert attention from spiritual themes. Sparking controversy with satirical wit, as in his essays that advocate closing the borders to further mass immigration and attack feminism,[1] he is not thought of as a writer on spiritual topics, unless as an antagonist. He is hostile to many forms of religious belief and practice, as typified in these aphorisms:

> Christian theology: nothing so grotesque could possibly be true.
> The gurus come from the sickliest nation on earth to tell us how to live. And we pay them for it.
> Belief in the supernatural reflects a failure of the imagination.[2]

No wonder his sometimes sophisticated and often sophomoric antireligious witticisms, combined with his attacks on environmentally damaging social and political activities and policies, interfere with readers' understanding of his spiritual complexity. Engaged with his essays on immigration and feminism in *One Life at a Time, Please*, for example, readers overlook the book's epigraph, which is an excerpt from the St. Francis of Assisi prayer:

O Lord, make me an instrument of thy peace.
Where there is hatred, let me sow love;
where there is darkness, light; and where
there is sadness, joy . . .

The essentials of Abbey's spiritual insight are that love, light, and joy are possible, despite the seductions of despair. If one is true to the earth, resisting doctrinaire religion and going beyond normal science, one is transformed by a beauty that transfigures the spirit. (He calls such a person an "earthiest.") Encounters with the desert and writing about them, the essentials of Abbey's creative life, brought spiritual awakenings that were antidotes to his despair.

Abbey grew up on a small Appalachian farm in Pennsylvania during the thirties and forties and moved west after wartime army service for his education. The move allowed him to combine twin passions for the mysterious desert and for philosophical inquiry. Besides Krutch's playfulness and joyfulness, Krutch's rationality inspired Abbey's admiration. For Abbey, Krutch was on the side of the best elements of "progress" and "civilization" and belonged in the company of, among others, "Mann, Tolstoy, Kropotkin, Camus, Russell, William O. Douglas, Lewis Mumford, Aldous and Julian Huxley." Krutch's contribution to this progressive strain of thinkers was "his communication of the discovery that the natural world must be treated as an equal partner" (*OL*, 180). Abbey, who died in 1989, aspired to be included in that tradition of thinkers about, and advocates of, "civilization."

Abbey did not like to be called a nature writer, even though most of his essays and novels are directly concerned with the natural environment (*JH*, xi–xiv). Who would blame him, since the reading public understands nature writing as a label for a genteel, if durable, literary occupation practiced by natural historians, and academics think of it as a minor literary tradition imitative of Thoreau? For them, Abbey writes, "Krutch and Abbey" are "Thoreaus of Arizona" (*AR*, xx). "I have not tried to write in their tradition," he claims, "I don't know how" (*JH*, xiii). Besides, he is puzzled "why so many want to read about the world out-of-doors, when it's more interesting simply to go for a walk into the heart of it" (*AR*, xviii, xxi).

The truth is that Abbey is to be included among the "sons and daughters of Thoreau," and he admits to sharing company with Joseph Wood Krutch, Edward Hoagland, Wendell Berry, and Annie Dillard, among others (*AR*, xx). Ann Ronald, in her study of Abbey's place among these writers, emphasizes his common interests with Thoreau and those who followed his lead, especially John Muir, John Wesley Powell, Mary Austin, and Joseph Wood Krutch. Abbey shared with Krutch, she summarizes, "a thirst for solitude, a love for the desert scene, a distrust of mechanized growth, a need for the desert's space."[3] His central connection with all these writers, Ronald notes, is "his respect for nature's inherent energy" and

> a belief in wilderness as a necessity for life, a dismay at inroads (in the name of progress) man has made against the land, a conviction that man must respect the earth's sacred energy and so must reverse the present trend toward growth at any cost, an unwavering love for what is wild.[4]

Peter Fritzell, too, admires Abbey's work within the nature-writing genre. The Edward Abbey in *Desert Solitaire* is for Fritzell "a prototypical figure in American nature writing—who finds the discord between nature and culture very much, too much, within himself."[5]

Even though we must include Edward Abbey among the most important twentieth-century nature writers, the other "sons and daughters of Thoreau" are more optimistic than Abbey. Joseph Wood Krutch had written in his first of many nature essays about experiencing absolute joy at hearing the "spring peepers" announcing a rebirth of the season and a rebirth of the human spirit as he intuits that "we are all in this together" just as Annie Dillard, for instance, ends *Pilgrim at Tinker Creek* with Christian optimism, saying "I go my way, and my left foot says 'Glory,' and my right foot says 'Amen' " (279). Moreover, it is only fair to Abbey as well as revealing to the reader to accept his invitation, more indirectly than directly offered, to place him within a broader literary lineage of writers he idolized: Mark Twain, Walt Whitman, Theodore Dreiser, and John Steinbeck. For Abbey, they were foremost critics of society who had faith in the evidence of their senses and used them to promote resistance to the state's power and injustices.[6] He adopted as his motto the phrase from Whitman "Resist much, obey little," and a passage Abbey quoted from Whitman captures the range of Abbey's literary objectives as well as outlines the larger literary community he aspired to join:

> This is what you shall do. Love the earth and the sun and the animals. Despise riches. Give alms to everyone that asks. Stand up for the stupid and crazy. Devote your income and labor to others, hate tyrants, have patience and indulgence toward the people, take off your hat to nothing known or unknown, or to any man or any number of men, go freely with powerful uneducated persons and the young and with the mothers of families. . . . Re-examine all you have been told at school or church or in any book and dismiss whatever insults your own soul. (*OL*, 175)

Edward Abbey, then, has an affinity with literary forebears who did not write nature essays and who struggle with views of the human and natural condition that are usually darker than those associated with nature essay writing. So far, critics have seen no merit in discussing that affinity with those writers. That there is merit in doing so can be demonstrated by accepting Abbey's invitation made through many allusions in his essays to the works of Jack London, Robinson Jeffers, and B. Traven. The reasons for Abbey's identification with them are personal, philosophical, political, and literary. Their confrontation and struggles with the bleakest aspects of experience help explain why Abbey describes his own writings as "antidotes to despair" (*DR*, 3).

Although Abbey is not explicit about the connections, he undoubtedly identifies with Jack London's life and work for many personal reasons. The two men's biographies match at many key points. In his biographical asides, Abbey emphasizes his childhood on an impoverished Appalachian farm, his youthful hoboing across the country, his night in jail, his attraction to anarchist ideas, and his wide experience as a profes-

sional writer. All resemble London's working-class background, adolescent experiences "on the road"—including a
night in a Buffalo, New York, jail for vagrancy—active socialist
involvement, and commitment to writing stories, novels, essays, and journalistic articles on a variety of social, political,
and economic topics. Both celebrate the world of masculine adventure in which violence is normative. Both have taken as
their basic literary mission the didactic one of conveying what
London called "strong truths" that others would repress for
political reasons.[7] Both proudly, even defiantly, announce
their stance as professional, working writers (*OL*, 161). And
both are criticized for contradictions, superficialities, and, at
times, sexism and racism in their writings. It has been said of
Abbey, as of London, "At times he is complex, deep, philosophical, and wise. At other times he is shallow, cynical, or
cruel; and he visits most of the way stations between."[8]

Abbey says that Jack London, rather than our contemporary John McPhee, author of the best-selling *Coming into the
Country* (1977), has written the "best book about Alaska"—*The
Call of the Wild*. "In the words of a critic," Abbey says, "Jack
London captures there the essence of the mythos of the wilderness."[9] Readers of London's northland novels and stories
know the central role of that mythos in London's works, a role
the desert Southwest and other exotic and demanding environ-
ments play in Abbey's essays and novels.[10] Tempted by philosophical nihilism, troubled by bleakness of spirit, and drifting
toward personal disaster, even suicide, London felt a call to adventure. "Something whispered . . . at the back of my consciousness," he wrote, that kept him alive.[11] Individually and
collectively, London's stories and novels depicting hazardous
journeys into the wilderness evoke an Alaskan landscape that
threatens protagonists with irrationality and death on one
hand and riches of the spirit on the other. The solitary figure in
the landscape is brought to the edge of the abyss, at which
point he is either broken or discovers a link with life beyond
anything that can be imagined in civilization. Similarly, Abbey's works—whether the classically conceived "season in the
wilderness journal," *Desert Solitaire*, or collections of essays
with such telling titles as *The Journey Home* (1977), *Abbey's Road*

(1979), *Down the River* (1982), and *Beyond the Wall* (1984)—are haunted by the threat of despair met by questing until one stares into the abyss and comes to terms with life. Remember, for instance, the passage from "Coda: Cape Solitude" in which Abbey literally stares into an isolated canyon abyss and has despair altered to "a roaring affirmation of existence" (*AR*, 195). Sounding in another place like the Jack London of "The White Silence," Abbey, hiking in the desert wilderness, acknowledges that "alone in the silence, I understand for a moment the dread which many feel in the presence of primeval desert" that comes from a threat greater than its danger or hostility—"its implacable indifference" (*DS*, 216). But having accepted that reality and endured the ordeal gives him a look "through God's window into eternity" (217).

Ann Ronald has written about this romantic element in Abbey's work. Although she makes no connection with London's writings, she might as well have been writing about both writers as she identifies in *Desert Solitaire* "Ed's" attraction to the abyss, his evocation of "the hostile indifference of the universe" and the threat of death, as he is "locating himself in the natural wasteland of the twentieth century."[12]

Ronald describes Abbey in *Desert Solitaire* as trying to be "rational, sensible and realistic" in order to "overcome at last that gallant infirmity of soul called romantic" only to succumb to "the deep spirit of the places." In the process there is a "three-step transfiguration of the land, from the literal to the metaphoric to the mythic" which Ronald links, through Northrop Frye's criticism, to Renaissance literature,[13] but which is more easily and clearly identified as characteristic of American literary naturalism in general and Jack London's fiction in particular.

More specific connections between the two men's outlooks can be seen in Abbey's essay "Fire Lookout: Numa Ridge" in *The Journey Home*. Once a lookout in a remote section of northwestern Montana's Glacier National Park, Abbey describes himself as a man with the "melancholy nature" prerequisite for such isolation, and he ponders present dangers and past suffering. To raise his spirits on this "cold, dismal, rain- and snow-soaked mountain" when he is so lonely and close to despondency that in his inner landscape looms "Mount Despair," he builds a fire in the "cold darkness of the lookout cabin" (56). The next day, his last as lookout, he thinks about the deer on the mountain in terms similar to those in Jack London's "Law of Life." In that London story the abandoned old Indian Koos-koosh sits by a dying fire, remembering how wolves pulled down an encircled moose. He understands that he, like the moose, must obey the Darwinian law of life to propagate the species so that it can survive even though the individual doesn't.[14] Of the deer at Numa Ridge, Abbey thinks,

> Danger everywhere. . . . A tough life. Always hard times for deer. The struggle for existence. All their energy goes into survival—and reproduction. The only point of it all—to go on. On and on and on. What else is there? Sometimes I am appalled by the brutality, the horror of this planetary spawning and scheming and striving and dying. One no longer searches for any ulterior significance in all this; as in the finest music, the meaning is in the music itself, not in anything beyond it. All we have, it seems to me, is the beauty of art and nature and life, and the love which that beauty inspires. (57)

Abbey looks into the abyss and, in effect, raises the old Indian's and London's question in "The Law of Life": "What does it matter after all?"

Abbey goes beyond London to an affirmation of this world's beauty, natural and created, that inspires a love of life; but here as elsewhere, Abbey's nature is Darwinian—dangerous, violent, brutal, killing—rather than the post-Darwinian nature of, say, Aldo Leopold or Joseph Wood Krutch, which more often emphasizes the fragile, benign, and life-sustaining. Moreover, as the quotation suggests, the nature Abbey observed, like London's, is a nature apprehended by sensual experience and analyzed rationally—in short, nature as understood by late nineteenth-century science. "There is more charm in one 'mere' fact, confirmed by test and observation, linked to other facts through coherent theory into a rational system, than in a whole brainful of fancy and fantasy. I see more poetry in a chunk of quartzite than in a make-believe wood nymph," writes Edward Abbey, sounding like Jack London as hard-boiled literary naturalist waging war against decadent, popular literary romanticism.[15] Science, not mysticism, is Abbey's guide. Abbey writes that "men like Democritus, Copernicus, Kepler, Newton, Lyell, Darwin, and Einstein" are "liberators of the human consciousness" who "have expanded our awareness of existence infinitely more than all the pronouncements of all the shamans, gurus, seers, and mystics of the earth, East and West, combined."[16]

It is the combination of emphasizing "fact" and—through adventuring—giving fact emotional and spiritual significance in a threatening Darwinian world that most completely matches Abbey's world view and writing with London's rather than with those of contemporary nature writers. All nature writers use facts, of course, as springboards to emotional experience and often mystical insight, and frequently record them with poetic diction. Jack London, however, wanted to combine harsh fact with "the stinging things of the spirit" through the adventures of a "spirit-groping and soul-searching" hero who would find "things wonderful."[17] Adventuring in that dangerous, Darwinian world is the way to treasures of the spirit for Abbey was well as London. "I, too, would have gone with the Forty-Niners," Abbey confesses in "Fool's Treasure." "Who cares whether we found true gold or only fool's gold? The adventure lies in the search, whether today, tomorrow or in 'Those days of old, / Those days of gold, / The days of forty-nine . . . ' " (*DR*, 171). The adventure gives significance to the harsh physical reality and brings the adventurer into contact with "something in the soul of the place, the spirit of the whole" that science cannot capture empirically and that "cannot be fully assimilated by the human imagination" (*JH*, 86). Similarly, London's adventurer "must understand the ways of the northland so sympathetically that he can anticipate its emergencies before they occur, always adapting himself to nature's laws, never attempting foolishly to impose the frail, devious customs of society and civilization upon the inviolable wilderness."[18]

There is, then, a romantic element in both London and Abbey that neither writer admits to respecting, even at times tries to deny; it is an emphatically mystical capacity stimulated by encountering the "unknowable" in London's northland or its equivalent, the "mystery" in Abbey's canyonlands. London's Alaskan landscape is the "unknowable," a term he borrowed from Herbert Spencer's *First Principles* (1876), and it cannot be comprehended through positivistic logic.[19] The protagonists of London's northland fiction learn "the absurdity of the finite contemplating the infinite."[20] In the American desert, Abbey encounters "mystery," his equivalent to God and grace. In the essay "The Ancient Dust," he writes that he experiences "something more in the desert. . . . I might call it a mystery—or simply Mystery itself, with an emphatically capital M . . . a sort of treasure. A kind of delight. God? Perhaps. Gold? Maybe. Grace? Possibly. But something a little more, a little different, even from these."[21] This romantic impulse, though, is grounded in harsh natural facts and, for the Abbey of *Desert Solitaire*, a nature that is better than people, as he rejoices darkly that humans are excluded from complete knowledge. "Why confuse the issue by dragging in a superfluous entity?" he asks. It is enough to "be true to the earth." Refusing the label "atheist," he says, "I am . . . an earthiest" (*DS*, 208).

Jack London never took the biocentric position—that all nature whether animate or inanimate is equal to humans—that characterizes Abbey's brand of religious feeling. One of the "strong truths" Abbey conveys is the egotism of anthropocentrism and the release found in biocentricity, the recognition that human life is not the centerpiece of existence and that wild nature offers us the chance to learn redemptive humility. His best passages from *Desert Solitaire* articulate this idea and bracket the volume at beginning and end. Concluding his account of his first morning in Utah's Canyonlands, he writes:

> The personification of the natural is exactly the tendency I wish to suppress in myself, to eliminate for good. I am here not only to evade for a while the clamor and filth and confusion of the cultural apparatus but also to confront, immediately and directly if it's possible, these bare bones of existence, the elemental and fundamental, the bedrock which sustains us. I want to be able to look at and into a juniper tree, a piece of quartz, a vulture, a spider, and see it as it is in itself, devoid of all humanly ascribed

qualities, anti-Kantian, even the categories of scientific description. To meet God or Medusa face to face, even if it means risking
everything human in myself. I dream of a hard and brutal mysticism in which the naked self merges with a non-human world
and yet somehow survives still intact, individual, separate. Paradox and bedrock. (*DS*, 6)

Critic Edward Twining responds: "Echoes, or course, of
Thoreau."[22] Yes, but it is as much, or more, a conscious echo of
Robinson Jeffers, the California poet of just such "a hard and
brutal mysticism."[23] His poem "Credo" announces that Jeffers
has gone beyond the mysticism of the Eastern religious practitioner who "believes that nothing is real except as we make it"
to find "a harder mysticism" in which "the ocean is the / bone
vault is only / The bone vault's ocean: out there is the ocean's: /
The water is the water, the cliff is the rock." [24] Similarly, Abbey's mysticism accepts the objective world as real, more en-
during, and worthy of more concern than human subjectivity;
it has nothing to do with the supernatural. London's "facts"
and Jeffers's rock, cliffs, and ocean are sufficient for Abbey. "I
am pleased enough with surfaces—in fact they alone seem to
me to be of much importance," Abbey writes in his introduction to *Desert Solitaire* (xiii). He will deal with mere appearances, with the surface of things. Abbey's stance is one that
Krutch and Jeffers would understand. Krutch, in an essay
about "how to see" the desert, asserted that "what I am after is
less to meet God face to face than really to take in a beetle, a
frog, or a mountain when I meet one."[25] In the concluding lines
of *Desert Solitaire* in the chapter "Bedrock and Paradox," referring to the long passage quoted above, Abbey again echoes
Robinson Jeffers: "The finest quality of this stone, these plants
and animals, this desert landscape is the indifference manifest
to our presence, our absence, our coming, our staying or our
going. Whether we live or die is a matter of absolutely no concern whatsoever to the desert" (267). These lines also capture
the essence of Jeffers's often discussed principle of "inhumanism."

While Jeffers's inhumanism has a tormented side bleaker
and more savage than anything found in Abbey's work, the

California poet's initial statement concerning his philosophy of inhumanism is consonant with Abbey's view. In the preface to *The Double Axe and Other Poems* (1948) Jeffers comments that his poem "The Love and the Hate," as well as some of his earlier work, presents "a certain philosophical attitude, which might be called Inhumanism, a shifting of emphasis and significance from man to not man; the rejection of human solipsism and recognition of the transhuman magnificence" (vii). Given to provocative statements affirming this "inhumanist," biocentric view, which unseats humans from their privileged place in creation, both Jeffers and Abbey have antagonized readers with similar lines. In "Hurt Hawks" Jeffers writes, "I'd sooner, except the penalties, kill a man than a hawk"; and Abbey in *Desert Solitaire* writes in playful allusion to Jeffers's line that "I have personal convictions to uphold. Ideals, you might say. I prefer not to kill animals. I'm a humanist; I'd rather kill a *man* than a snake" (could he have meant "I am an inhumanist"?).[26] And both men concentrate on aspects of nature that are least easily personified, "the beauty of inanimate things" found on the rocky coastline of Big Sur or the desert wilderness of sand and canyons. In this, they contrast with other nature writers who, like Thoreau at Walden Pond or Annie Dillard at Tinker Creek, are most attuned to animate nature.[27] In a nature that is massive and inanimate in its most telling features, away from cities and the corrupted culture of people in the aggregate, Abbey—as did Jeffers—experiences redemptive beauty.

Abbey distances himself from Jeffers's humorless and bitter misanthropy. Misanthropy, after all, is not a requirement of "inhumanism" even by Jeffers's own definition. It requires a shift in "emphasis and significance" from man to not-man, not a replacement of man with non-man. As poet and critic Diane Wakoski concludes, Abbey's "inhumanism" differs from Jeffers's because "there is no real conviction here that all humanity is a mistake. . . . Not that mankind is bad. Only that certain humans are, and that in large numbers humankind is trouble" (*RM*, 106). Abbey could admire Jeffers but not love him (*OL*, 72).

Nevertheless, major features of Abbey's and Jeffers's world views coincide. Jeffers's response to charges of pessimism are, in fact, not so different from Abbey's responses to his own impulses toward despair. In the same passage in which Jeffers defines his inhumanism, for instance, he states that despite charges against it, this "manner of thought and feeling is neither misanthropic nor pessimist" because "it provides magnificence for the religious instinct, and satisfies our need to admire greatness and rejoice in beauty."[28] Abbey, for his part, turns to a wilderness that at times places crushing demands upon body and spirit because there he most completely engages the enlivening "mystery" required by his religious instinct and he can rejoice in beauty. Summarizing his reasons for writing in "A Writer's Credo," Abbey states, in words that recall Jeffers's, that he does so, in part, "to praise the divine beauty of the natural world," startling words from a writer who, like Jeffers, is often thought of as inclined toward nihilism (*OL*, 178).

The threat of nihilism is, of course, present in both men's works. Abbey's and Jeffers's response to it is more angry and aggressive than Leopold's and Krutch's doubt and stoicism. The anger is there, for example, in the social and political views Abbey and Jeffers share. For Abbey, the object of writing is "to defend the diversity and freedom of human kind from those forces in our techno-industrial culture that would reduce us all, if we let them, to the status of things, objects, raw material, personnel; the rank of subjects" (*AR*, xiii). He says he needs to write to overcome a brush with "nothingness" by communicating to others "what would be intolerable to bear alone" (xxiii). And Abbey salutes Robinson Jeffers as an early twentieth-century Jeremiah against the ravages of mechanized, urban man. Abbey made a pilgrimage to Jeffers's Tor House and Hawk Tower home to honor "one of American's best, most reclusive, least known and most unpopular poets" who, Abbey knew, lived long enough (until 1962) to see his granite seaside home engulfed by the "progress" of the California real estate boom (*OL*, 71). Jeffers had early prophesied such desecration in poems like that from which Abbey quotes:

The extraordinary patience of things!
This beautiful place defaced with a crop of suburban houses —
How beautiful when we first beheld it.
Unbroken field of poppy and lupine walled with clean cliffs,
No intrusion but two or three horses pasturing . . .
Now the spoiler has come; does it [the place] care?
Not faintly. It has all time. It knows the people are a tide
That swells and in time will ebb, and all
Their works dissolve . . .[29]

Abbey, too, believes that people in the aggregate have been corrupted by a technological culture that has pushed westward and now even into the desert wilderness. He himself envisions a future when wilderness areas will be necessary retreats for guerrillas warring against an American totalitarian state already in the making; then he announces, "It was all foreseen nearly half a century ago by the most cold-eyed and clear-eyed of our national poets, on California's shore, at the end of the open road. Shine, perishing republic." The last sentence, of course, is the title of the famous Jeffers poem published more than sixty years earlier.[30] Both Abbey and Jeffers had apocalyptic sensibilities and inclinations to write jeremiads.

While Abbey must be included among those who interpret Jeffers as willing the extinction of mankind and who reject the position as too extreme, the two writers' historical views are very similar on key points. Jeffers's cyclical view is that "great civilizations have broken down into violence, and their tyrants / come, many times before" and will again, so he exhorts us to love "the divine beauty of the universe" apprehended in the "organic wholeness" of "life and things." "Love that, not man," he exhorts, "or else you will share man's pitiful confusions, / or drown in despair when his days darken."[31] In the "Episodes and Visions" chapter of *Desert Solitaire* Abbey is likeminded. Talking with a visitor, Abbey finds that he must defend his "desert thoughts" — his opposition to humanity, to scientism, and to culture. He discovers that he is, in his terminology, opposed to "culture" (mindless, destructive conformity, which he hopes is on the wane) rather than "civilization," to the worship of technology and technique ("scientism") rather than science, and to anthropocentricity ("the opinion that the world exists solely for the sake of man") rather than humankind (244–45). His optimism, against a background of greed, violence, cruelty, oppression, the routinized, and homogenized, is shown in his recovery of courage, freedom, and good humor. Abbey himself has seen that miracle happen at Trinity, New Mexico, where the first atomic bomb exploded. "Let men in their madness blast every city on earth into black rubble and envelop the entire planet in a cloud of lethal gas," Abbey writes in the "bedrock and paradox" passage so indebted to Jeffers (and biblical cadences), "the springs and rocks will still be here, the sunlight will filter through, water will form and warmth shall be upon the land and after sufficient time, no matter how long, somewhere, living things will emerge and join and stand once again" (267). He parts company with Jeffers, however, hoping that "this time perhaps" the living things will take "a different and better course." In the face of doubt and nihilistic temptation, that hope is his "animal faith" (267). Elsewhere, also, Abbey's statements evoke Jeffers's historical views but edge away from nihilism and toward cautious affirmation.[32] He believes that "the industrial, military state will eventually collapse or destroy itself" and it may be true that "the worst possible future for the American West is already here." At his most affirmative, he states that "I still think it's possible to find some better way to live, both as an individual and as a society" (*RM*, 91).

It is difficult to tell just how deeply Abbey holds these social views because of the spontaneity of interviews and his propensity for playfulness. Nonetheless, it is safe to say that like Jeffers he has contempt for herd man, a vision of the inevitable collapse of decadent social-political structures, and a vision of the persistence of a beautiful and inspiring nature. Nature's beauty inspires the mysticism, albeit hard and brutal, through her "indifference," that prepares one to hear and embrace God if that is to happen (*AR*, 195). And if that doesn't happen, Abbey and Jeffers agree that we must "praise the divine beauty of the natural world" (Abbey) and witness "the divine beauty of the universe" (Jeffers).

While Abbey admired and drew from Robinson Jeffers and Jack London, he reserves his highest praise for a lesser-known writer. "My favorite 20th-century writer is B. Traven," Abbey told an interviewer in 1970.[33] Even adjusting for Abbey's taste for overstatement, there can be no doubt anarchist B. Traven, enigmatic author of *The Treasure of the Sierra Madre* (1936), is important to Abbey's sense of himself as writer. Direct allusions to Traven appear in Abbey's essays and novels: *The Journey Home, Good News, Down the River, One Life at a Time, Please,* and *The Fool's Progress.* The most obvious example of Traven's importance to Abbey's theme of despair and its antidotes is Abbey's allusion to Traven in *The Fool's Progress.*[34] Protagonist Henry Lightcap is experiencing not just pain but "the pain of pain" of his wife's having left him (26). Getting drunk, he prepares for "another long dark night of the soul" and remembers "her parting gift: despair" (7). He calls his doctor friend and asks for "real potent pills." Instead, the doctor prescribes turning on the television set since "they're showing *Treasure of Sierra Madre* on channel nine, best movie ever made" (11).

The prescription is actually to help Lightcap get in touch with essential values as he and Abbey's heroes know them. The way to knowledge for Abbey and Traven, as for Jack London, is through suffering endured during an odyssey through remote and demanding terrain. The settings of most Traven novels are harsh Mexican deserts and jungles, his equivalents to London's Alaskan wastelands and South Sea jungles. Within the larger literary framework of masculine adventure tales, the melancholy protagonists begin questing for treasure and end struggling for survival. Their daily experience is of pain barely endured.

If spirit-crushing and life-threatening landscapes are the settings and pain the central experience, Traven's subjects and themes are not about nature and environmentalism—they are more broadly social and political.[35] Given the substance and context of Abbey's allusions to Traven's work, clearly Abbey admires Traven because of his truthfulness about the suffering of ordinary people at the hands of greedy landowners, unchecked industrial capitalism, and abstracted bureaucracy. For instance, the epigraph to *Good News* (1980), Abbey's apocalyptic novel of the near future when fascists are controlling America and exercising their greed and amoral power, is from Traven's *March to Monteria* (1964): "This is the real world, muchachos, and you are

in it." In this Traven novel the Indians march through the pesti-
lent jungle to promised jobs that turn out to be slave labor, having
been tricked out of their wages and their hopes by plantation
owners and overseers. Abbey alludes to the same passage in
"Down There in Sonora": the "real world" is an "empire of industry and social combat" closing in on us inexorably (*DR*, 153).

Abbey shares with Traven the earlier writer's lifelong commitment to anarchism. The title of Abbey's master's degree thesis in philosophy at the University of New Mexico is "Anarchism and the Morality of Violence" (1959), and as late as 1987
he wrote an essay entitled "Theory of Anarchy" in which he
says simply, "Anarchism means maximum democracy" (*OL*, 25).
Collectively, Abbey's twenty books are "meditations on that un-
complicated moral and political vision" that "all governments . . .
must be abolished, to be replaced by self-rule and cooperativ-
ism."[36] Abbey opens his rollicking anarchist novel, *The Monkey
Wrench Gang*, with a quote from Byron: "Down with all Kings but
King Ludd." The novel is dedicated to the memory of "Ned
Ludd or *Lud* . . . a lunatic living about 1779, who in a fit of rage
smashed up two frames belonging to a Leicestershire 'stock-
inger' " and disrupted British industrialization for a while.

Not surprisingly, therefore, Abbey's favorite novel by his
favorite twentieth-century novelist is not *The Treasure of the Sierra Madre* but *The Death Ship* (1934), which is relentless in its
critique of modern life from the anarchist perspective. Subtitled
The Story of an American Sailor, *The Death Ship* is narrated by melancholy merchant seaman Gerald Gales, who fails to return before his ship leaves Belgium. Aboard ship are his identification
papers, leaving him without proof of national identity. Jailed
and deported, he is unable to secure help from American con-
suls in a succession of European countries and has no alternative but to join the crew of a "death ship" whose owners want
to scuttle it for insurance money. Brutal conditions aboard the
death ship are central to the novel; its sailors become the "mor-
ibund," the walking dead, even before drowning. Only Gales
survives. The themes are the staples of anarchism: Gales and
the other common seamen are victimized by nationalistic nar-
rowness, bureaucratic indifference, and capitalistic greed.

Throughout the ordeal and in his anguish, as Gales learns

these anarchist lessons about the ways of the world, he experiences a growing sense of futility. In despair, he asks, "Where is the true company of men?"[37] Abbey uses the same passage as the epigraph for the "Down There in Sonora" essay, which rails against the "empire of industry." Gales, in fact, goes on to answer his question. The true company of men is

> there where nobody molests me, where nobody wants to know who I am, where I come from, where I wish to go, what my opinion is about war, about the Episcopalians, and about the communists, where I am free to do and to believe what I damn please as long as I do not harm the life, the health, and the honestly earned property of anyone else.[38]

For Abbey, as for Traven, that place is in the anarchist's imagination rather than in the "real world" he and Traven dramatize in their fiction. Their joint literary mission, in Abbey's words, is "to oppose, resist, and sabotage the contemporary drift toward a global technocratic police state . . . to oppose injustice, to defy power, and to speak for the voiceless" (OL, 177–78). Even more simply, Abbey quotes Samuel Johnson, whose goal as a writer is " 'to make the world better' "(178).

There is a tension in both Abbey's and Traven's work between knowing what is wrong and making the world better, between knowledge and action. Gales and the various Abbey protagonists, including Ed in *Desert Solitaire*, are well informed about injustice but, as is characteristic of anarchists, have no program for reform or revolution. A temptation is, therefore, to become what Abbey calls the "ironical anarchist" who talks and thinks like an anarchist but acts like a good citizen—for example, Bondi in Abbey's *Brave Cowboy*. Even if a person acts, results may be ambiguous or of slight consequence, as are the futile actions of Jack Burns, "the brave cowboy," or as are the Monkey Wrench Gang's efforts in waging guerrilla war against developers in the Southwest. Satisfaction remains in the realm of intellect, imagination, and emotion—in naming and ridiculing the villains.

The ways Abbey and Traven do that naming and ridiculing are antidotes to despair. The authors mix suffering and outrage that are largely political, but not without metaphysical overtones, with slapstick comedy and extravagant fantasy. A comic narrative stance is the antidote to a melancholy that tends toward nihilism. The first person narrative of *The Death Ship* is filled with the wise-cracking tar's amusing accounts of his unrelieved disasters on land and sea. With the possibility of facing a French firing squad at dawn, Gales begs to be shot several times so that he can have several elegant last suppers (98–99). Another broadly comic set piece is Gales's account of his shipmate Stanislav's effort to establish his nationality and get proper papers. Because he was born in Posen, Prussia, which later became Posnan, Poland, and because in the interim he had sailed under various aliases and flags during peace and wartime, he had no bureaucratically acceptable evidence of his nationality. The chapter-long comic narrative of Stanislav's story becomes a wide-ranging anarchist satire of nationalism, capitalism, and bureaucracy (252–59).

Abbey, too, is given to broadly satirical comic gestures. For instance, during one of the frequent chase scenes in *The Monkey Wrench Gang*, George Washington Hayduke and Seldom Seen Smith pause by the roadside in public rangeland near the Utah-Arizona border to cut a barbed wire fence. Smith says, " 'You can't never go wrong cuttin' fence. . . . Always cut fence. That's the law of the hundredth meridian. East of that don't matter none. Back there it's all lost anyhow. But west, cut fence.' (*Plang!*)" (144). The same characters, including the Lone Ranger and others who planned to blow up Glen Canyon Dam, return in Abbey's posthumous novel, *Hayduke Lives!* (1990), to bedevil Bishop Love and his plans to use the megamachine GOLIATH that slouches toward public canyonlands to transform them into yet another deluxe motel and golf course with spectacular views. It is humor based in outrage, which is intellectually framed by Lewis Mumford's influential concept of the "megamachine" in *The Myth of the Machine* (1970), that associates complex technology with coercive bureaucracies and authoritarian hierarchies, including the military, economic, and political.[39] GOLIATH is obviously Abbey's symbol of technology's empowerment of centralized organizations over both human and natural communities. It is a comic symbol with rich intellectual associations.

Abbey's spokesmen consistently joke and take comic action

against a background of social and spiritual trouble. No wonder Abbey's list of his most admired contemporary writers and works includes "Kurt Vonnegut, humanist and humorist in the Mark Twain tradition," Rober Coover and his *Public Burning* about the Rosenberg atomic spy case, William Gaddis's *JR* satire of corporate America, and Thomas Pynchon's encyclopedic and comic exploration of the darkest side of the American psyche, *Gravity's Rainbow* (*OL*, 174).

The effect of the humorous tone in Traven's and Abbey's novels about suffering and injustice is to evoke tolerance for human limitations while castigating the worst practices and injustices arising from greed and hypocrisy. Imperfect individuals drawn to one another by their best qualities affirm the anarchist's faith that a passion for freedom and trust in mutual aid offer the best hope. While Abbey owes a debt to his Thoreauvian political heritage, just as he owes a debt to his Thoreauvian love of the natural world, it is just as clear that he owes and acknowledges a debt to B. Traven that is found in their shared political vision and literary strategies.

Relationships between Edward Abbey's writing and Earth First!, the most radical of American environmental groups, indicate that the line between knowing what is wrong and doing something about it has blurred. Roderick Nash claims with justification that *The Monkey Wrench Gang*'s "monkeywrenching" tactics became Earth First!'s "blueprint for action" (*RN*, 191). The organization adopted Abbey's radical biocentricity, extending the Christian ethic beyond humans "to include the living creatures that share the planet with us" and beyond to "the nonliving, the inorganic, to the springs, streams, very rocks which form the foundation of the land, [to] the hills, mountains, swamps, deserts, plains and seashores."[40] *Ecodefense: A Field Guide to Monkeywrenching* (second edition), a "Ned Ludd Book," is edited by Earth First!'s central figures, Dave Foreman and Bill Haywood, and dedicated to members of the Bonnie Abbzug Feminist Garden Club. Bonnie, of course, is a central character in *The Monkey Wrench Gang*. And Abbey himself contributes the foreword—entitled "Forward!"—urging readers to defend wilderness against "the greedy and powerful" minority by using the strategies, tactics, and techniques outlined in *Eco-*

defense (8–9). They include the now familiar actions of tree and road spiking, vehicle disabling, and billboard destruction, as well as information on how to avoid capture or, if that fails, how to be nice to cops.

Anarchist comedy continues in *Hayduke Lives!*, the sequel to *The Monkey Wrench Gang*. Fiction and ordinary life mix in comic proportions. In the chapter "Earth First! Rendezvous," such Earth First! familiars as Foreman and Haywood make appearances along with Abbey himself, and the narrator mentions many other environmentally important figures such as elder statesmen Aldo Leopold and Garrett Hardin, deep ecologists Arne Naess, George Sessions, and Bill Devall, earth ritualist Dolores LaChapelle, and poet environmentalist Gary Snyder (202–3). The chapter's opening is a masterpiece of foolery, a list of folk who have come to the Earth First! rendezvous. A partial list includes:

> the sober conservationist, the native American 1/16th Chippewa Mother Earth Goddess, the mountain man in buckskin with fringes, . . . the beer-drinking fun-loving gun-happy trailbusters in sweat-rich camouflage T-shirts . . . , the zealot-eyed unisexual fun-hating sectarian Marxists in corduroy and workman shirts, the pot-smoking flower kids sagging into middle age, Vietnam vets hiding in the woods, . . . misanthropic redneck pseudo-intellectuals steeped in Thoreau and Garrett Hardin, . . . Neanderthalian macho mystics, . . . and shifty numbers of spies and informers garishly disguised as 1960s hippies. (186–87)

These "Sagebrush Patriots" carry banners and flags that denounce the " 'oligarchical swine' " who " 'own and operate America' ":

> HUNT COWS, NOT BEARS . . .
> MALTHUS WAS RIGHT
> MUIR POWER TO YOU
> NATURE BATS LAST
> REDNECKS FOR WILDERNESS . . .
> THINK GLOBALLY — ACT LOCALLY
> SUBVERT THE DOMINANT PARADIGM
> (199–200)

They wave the "flag of anarchy, red monkey wrench on a field of black" (199). It is anarchist comedy, like B. Traven's, which celebrates flawed ordinary people who struggle against the rich and powerful to defend the earth, offering "No Compromise in Defense of Mother Earth" (Earth First!'s motto). "Humor, in Mr. Abbey's work," Wendell Berry concludes, "is a function of his outrage, and is therefore always answering to necessity. Without his humor, his outrage would be intolerable—as, without his outrage, his humor would often be shallow or self-exploitive" (*RM*, 11). And when using his comic powers to vent his social rage while writing in defense of nature and in opposition to the megamachine, Abbey is most clearly not a nature writer.

The numerous allusions throughout Edward Abbey's work to other writers such as Walt Whitman, Mark Twain, Theodore Dreiser, John Steinbeck, Nelson Algren, Wallace Stegner, William Gaddis, Thomas Pynchon, Robert Coover, Robert Stone, E. L. Doctorow, Joseph Heller, Kurt Vonnegut, William Kotzwinkle, and Thomas Berger—but especially to Jack London, Robinson Jeffers, and B. Traven—show that Abbey identifies himself with wider currents in American literary history than nature writing. Those writers, individually and in the aggregate, exhibit qualities at the heart of Abbey's own sense of literary mission. All emphasize the harsh realities of life in society and life in nature. Abbey, London, Jeffers, and Traven criticize the dominant culture for the damage it inflicts on ordinary people; they are political writers who unabashedly accept political subjects and themes as not only congenial to art but essential to it. Not only are the social worlds they create routinely marked with cruelty and injustice, but the natural world is the harsh Darwinian arena of struggle and violence.

Whether adventuring into that dangerous landscape as protagonists in London's and Traven's fiction or confronting it through Jeffers's poetry of inhumanism, humans are taken to the edge of the abyss of nihilism where they suffer spiritual, as much as physical, anguish. At the brink, these writers remain faithful to their common philosophical materialism but admit to engaging the "unknowable" or an organic wholeness, through direct and difficult encounters with the land, which, finally, radiates a beauty that transfigures the spirit. Edward Abbey's antidotes to despair—that is, his essays themselves, their narrative stances, the themes of suffering endured and transcended through adventure, and of escape from individual and collective egotism through biocentricity and anarchist hope— substantiate his claim to broader kinships among American literary figures than with nature writers only.

He does, without question, however, also belong with writers primarily concerned with nature, American writers like Joseph Wood Krutch who are philosophically committed to science but who yearn also for spiritual experiences that science cannot provide. He belongs with those like Annie Dillard who have turned toward the natural world as a guide to personal and spiritual values on the one hand and relief from the burdens of self on the other. And he belongs with writers like Gary Snyder who angrily call attention to self-inflicted social deterioration and violent acts against the natural world while exploring radical political assessments and alternatives. Edward Abbey, self-described Earthiest, enjoins us to "be true to the earth," defends Mother Earth, as do his environmental anarchist "eco-warriors" in *Hayduke Lives!*, and finds safety both literally and imaginatively by trekking "into the secret hidden inner world of canyon and desert."[41]

5
Annie Dillard: Ritualist

Why art thou cast down, O my soul? and why art thou disquieted
within me? hope thou in God: for I shall yet praise him, who is the
health of my countenance, and my God.
— (Psalm 42)

From the dark mouth of the burrow, under the far bank of the frozen
stream, tracks led away over the ice. I longed to follow them around a
distant bend in the stream. But the reaches beyond, forbidding under
the still tenseness of the ominous sky, slowed my steps to a standstill.
However, my mind and imagination were racing.
— Edwin Way Teale (1945)

When Edward Abbey wrote that "sons and daughters of Thoreau abound in contemporary American writing," listing Edward Hoagland, Joseph Wood Krutch, Wendell Berry, John
McPhee, Ann Zwinger, and Peter Matthiessen, as well as himself, he reserved his highest praise for Annie Dillard, who "is
the true heir of the Master" (AR, xx). The others are Thoreauvian primarily, says Abbey, in their identification with special
locales — from Central Park in Hoagland's essays to Zwinger's
Rockies. But Dillard, the Thoreau of Tinker Creek, Virginia,
and Puget Sound, "alone has been able to compose, successfully, in Thoreau's extravagant and transcendental manner."
Abbey's one objection to Dillard's "otherwise strong, radiant
book [Pilgrim at Tinker Creek] is the constant name dropping. Always of one name" — God (AR, xx). His assessment is astute because it highlights the essential characteristics of Annie Dillard's nature writing: her writing about place, the language she
uses to evoke her experiences, and her religious preoccupation
and vocation. But Abbey's assessment is also eccentric because
his objection to her religious preoccupation is directed at Dillard's most distinctive achievements in the nature essays of *Pil-*

guitars" and likens her attendance to having "run away from home and joined the circus as a dancing bear" (18–19).

At times she strains to remain Christian, as in *Holy the Firm* when she rejects pantheistic immanence, that "God is in the thing," referred to above, but cannot quite accept the conventional Christian view that "emanating from God, and linked to him by Christ, the world is infinitely other than God" (73). While the concept of emanation (Christ originating directly from Godhead rather than nature) permits a representation of Christ which allows for the salvation of "the souls of men," it leaves the rest of nature "irrelevant and nonparticipant," unreal to time," "unknowable, an illusory, absurd, accidental, and overelaborate stage"—in a word, fallen (74). Unwilling to accept a view that denies a sacralized familiar natural world, she entertains a view from "esoteric Christianity" that there is a substance called "Holy the Firm," which is "in touch" with both the lowest of material reality—the "salts and earths"—and the Absolute (72). The Absolute and the most ordinary aspects of nature are connected, "matter and spirit are of a piece but distinguishable; God has a stake guaranteed in all the world" (75). Characteristically, Dillard undercuts her affirmations, this time with an anticlimactic aside that "these are only ideas" (75). Nevertheless, for Dillard there is no such thing as "only" ideas. In all her writing she proves herself outside orthodoxy and beyond conventional Christianity without abandoning Christian preoccupations, beliefs, and longings.

As Reimer has shown, Dillard's "theology is always dialectical, contain(ing) both the conventional language of religious mysticism as well as more macabre elements of religious experiences" (187). The dialectical tension is between "the material and the spiritual, the natural and the transcendent . . . the beauty and the horror within the natural world" (182). She concludes that "the power of Dillard's vision arises from her strength to maintain the contradictions within a single vision" (189).

Dillard's vision is contradictory at its most extreme and dialectical in its most powerful insights. To balance these unresolved contradictions within a single, unified vision, she creates rituals that are familiar to both religious practitioners and nature observers.

Students of myth and ritual know that world views, or myths, contain contradictions and unresolved mysteries that adherents live with despite doubt. Aldo Leopold's mythic stance in A Sand County Almanac encourages a new sense of relations between humans and nature and urges us toward a new state of ethical awareness and conduct even in the face of unresolved dilemmas about both nature (known and unknown), human motives (love and greed), and public land policy (protection and mismanagement). Ritual is a way both of moving toward deeper understanding and of affirming belief publicly, a way of acting without complete knowledge, of getting beyond the empirical and rational. Annie Dillard seeks a vision that is "the pearl of great price" that "may be found" but "may not be sought," so the question becomes "how then is she to act? How is the search to be conducted?"[13] Annie Dillard's ritual acts allow her to affirm life and God without a theological resolution of fundamental religious questions. Through these rituals she strives for—and experiences—reconciliation between herself, a sometimes horrible—as well as beautiful—nature, and a mysterious God who at times seems as maniacal as loving. Fittingly, her rituals blend Judeo-Christian rites and language with her own private rites in nature; they are the rituals of stalking, seeing, and dancing.

Walkers are pilgrims seeking visions. Walking as more than exercise has a long tradition in literature, from Plato's walks during which he formulated his dialogues, to Saint Augustine's walk on the seashore, to seventeenth-century literary figures who walked as a form of Christian meditation, to Romantic walkers William Wordsworth, Henry David Thoreau, and John Muir. Tom Wolf, field biologist and walker, notes that for seventeenth-century Christian literary walkers "the walk is an occasion and setting for revelation, for a sudden increase in their awareness of the indwelling of God in the world."[14] Or, as Thoreau comments in "Walking," those few who understand "the art of Walking," who "have a genius for *sauntering*" (his italics) are linked with medieval pilgrims about whom children exclaimed, " 'There goes a saunterer,' a Holy-Lander." Those who walk in Thoreau's way "saunter toward the Holy Land, till one day the sun shall shine more brightly than ever he has done, shall perchance shine into our minds and hearts, and light up our whole lives with a great awakening light, as warm and serene and golden as on a bankside in autumn."[15] Thoreau's imagery of light appears in Dillard's mystical moments as, indeed, in all of the mystical tradition, including the Christian. John Elder writes that for inveterate walker William Wordsworth, the "Pilgrim" of "The Prelude," "walking is a process of reconciliation: it provides the dynamic unity of his life" and art. "The Prelude," for example, is a work organized in part by the rhythms of walking. Elder, in ways applicable to Dillard's essays, writes about walking in the works of other writers, such as contemporary poet A. R. Ammons. Writing about Ammons, he might as well be writing about Dillard: "There is no absolute unity available for existence in a physical, and thus temporal, world. Rather, going from one foot to the other, human life takes its passage through a universe of particulars," and the major response to the relations between nature, human imagination, and spirit is "one of ambivalence: right foot, left foot."[16]

For Dillard, as for many other seekers, walking is superficially casual; but it is true ritual, a common action become uncommon, a preparation for metaphysical experience rather than the merely social or moral. Thus, Dillard does not just walk; she stalks the natural object, and she stalks the metaphysical.

In the *Pilgrim at Tinker Creek* chapter entitled "Stalking," Dillard tells us she learned to stalk fish and muskrats who "by their very mystery and hiddenness crystallize the quality of my summer life at the creek" (188). Learning to stalk muskrats took "several years" until one evening, when she had "lost" herself, "lost the creek, the day, lost everything but [the creek's] amber depth," a young muskrat "appeared on top of the water, floating on its back" (194). She is ecstatic. The excitement and wonder of sighting an "ordinary" muskrat through her ritual stalking is described with the language of revelation: she records her joy and surprise "at having the light come on so suddenly, and at having my consciousness returned to me all at once and bearing [a] . . . muskrat" (194). Fearing that encounter was a once in a lifetime experience, she stalks muskrats day and night; and when she witnesses another muskrat, she reports, with the Thoreauvian extravagance Edward Abbey so admired, that "my life changed" (195). What Dillard calls stalking is, obviously, meditational practice. The *"via negative,"* she says, is a form of stalking that lets her become "Newton under the apple tree, Buddha under the bo" (187). Certainly Gary Snyder, whose poem "A Walk" signifies that both walking and writing are Buddhist practices, would agree, knowing as essayist Gretel Ehrlich learned that "the word 'walk' in Japanese can also refer to Buddhist practice" and that "the further the sojourner walk[s] from discursive mind and habitual thought, the closer she or he came back to original nature, to the 'Buddha nature' within."[17] Recalling Ezekiel's excoriation of false prophets who feared pursuing God into dangerous places, Dillard exhorts us to "stalk the gaps" in "altitudes and latitudes so dazzlingly spare and clean that the spirit can discover itself for the first time like a once-blind man unbound." Such stalking will reveal, she writes, "more than a maple"; it will reveal "a universe" (276).

Her walks around Tinker Creek in Virginia and her stalking of the muskrat, then, reveal not merely the habits of the secretive animal, for the mystery and hiddenness she often attributes to muskrats are those she most often attributes to God. Moreover, her personal ritual of stalking is ultimately described in Christian terms: on the night her life changes dramatically as a result of witnessing the muskrat, she summarizes the nature of the stalking ritual as "Knock; seek; ask," obviously a variant of the biblical "Ask, and it shall be given you; seek, and ye shall find; knock, and it shall be opened to you. For everyone that asketh receiveth; and he that seeketh findeth; and to him that knocketh it shall be opened" (195). In Dillard the nature-writing conventions of encountering nature directly and immediately through ordinary activities such as walking, while—necessarily—one is open to aesthetic and spiritual experience, mingle and meld with Christian ritual, tradition, and experience. Ordinary experience fuses with the millennial, the temporal with the transcendent.

In *Holy the Firm* and *Teaching a Stone to Talk,* Dillard persistently, if less obviously, uses the walking ritual emphasized in *Pilgrim at Tinker Creek*. In *Holy the Firm*, for instance, she is deeply troubled by the terrible suffering of Julie Norwich, who is hospitalized, her face burned in a plane accident. Agonizing over the Christian response to the sufferings of the innocent, Dillard, near despair, asks, "Do we really need more victims to remind us that we're all victims?" (62). Sounding very much like the radically alienated Joseph Wood Krutch of *Modern Temper*, she reminds herself that we are "sojourners in a land we did not make, a land with no meaning of itself and no meaning we can make for it alone" (63). In this state of mind, she feels unworthy to buy the communion wine she had volunteered to get, but goes anyway. She walks home, "and I'm on the road again walking, my right hand forgetting my left. I'm out on the road again walking, and toting a backload of God" (66). As she starts up a hill, the landscape starts "to utter its infinite particulars," and she lists particular features of the landscape about her—"blackberry brambles, white snowberries, red rose hips, gaunt and clattering broom" (67). Soon, the particulars are alive: "mountains are raw nerves; . . . the trees, the grass . . . are living petals of mind." Finally, "walking faster and faster, weightless, I feel the wine. It sheds light in slats through my rib cage, and fills the buttressed vaults of my ribs with light pooled and buoyant. I am moth; I am light. I am prayer and I can hardly see" (68). At that moment, she experiences the vision that is central to *Holy the Firm*; she beholds Christ being baptized.

The essays in *Teaching a Stone to Talk* often extend the notion of ordinary walking to large journeys and expeditions. In "Sojourner" she notes that the title word appears frequently in the Old Testament and "invokes a nomadic people's sense of vagrancy, a praying people's knowledge of estrangement, a thinking people's intuition of sharp loss" (150). Thus, in this essay as well as in her writing generally, she alternates between "thinking of the planet as home" and "as a hard land of exile in which we are all sojourners" (150). A number of the essays in *Teaching a Stone to Talk* explore the dialectic between being at home and being estranged, a motif that is explicit in Abbey's *Journey Home* themes, implicit in Leopold's central image of his

Sand County farm on wounded land, in Krutch's change of geographical and spiritual addresses from New York City to Tucson, and in Snyder's advocacy of bioregionalism and personal commitment to Kitkitdizze, his home in the Sierra foothills of northern California or, as he prefers, in Shasta Nation. In *Teaching a Stone to Talk*, Dillard moves her settings from Tinker Creek to places as remote as the North Pole and the Napo River in the Ecuadorian jungle.

In "An Expedition to the Pole," she combines personal experience, history, and fantasy. The personal experience of visiting the Arctic and viewing the Arctic Sea fuses with the history of various polar expeditions that entailed enormous suffering for ill-equipped explorers. She fantasizes that she has "quit my ship and set out on foot over the polar ice," traveling across an ice floe where she encounters both historical personages and members of the congregation of the Catholic church she has been attending. They are all together on a spiritual quest. Her attendance at Catholic services is part of her search for "the Pole of Relative Inaccessibility," or in other words, "The Absolute" (19). She asks "How often have I mounted this same expedition, has my absurd barque set out half-caulked for the Pole?" Seeking to define her aim and strategy, she quotes Pope Gregory, who stated the aim of spiritual expeditions as attaining " 'to somewhat of the unencompassed light, by stealth' " (44). Although Dillard emphasizes alienated experience because she is so poorly and absurdly equipped for her spiritual expedition to the Pole, she ends the essay with a fantasy as exuberant as any of Edward Abbey's in which she is on the floe with the church members, "banging on a tambourine" and singing loudly. "How can any of us tone it down?" she asks, "for we are nearing the Pole" (52). Dillard actually seeks and creates the conditions for ecstatic, mystical experience; doubt and hope are held in balance within the imaginative framework of sojourning, of exploring on foot.

Annie Dillard walks and stalks so that she can "see" in more than one sense. To see truly, she must prepare herself ritualistically, must become both innocent and informed.

For Dillard innocence is "the spirit's unself-conscious state at any moment of pure devotion to any object. It is at once a receptiveness and total concentration" (*PTC*, 83). Innocence is a state she values as highly as did romantics and Christians before her, a state similar, even, to the one Krutch aspires to so he can "take in a beetle, a frog, or a mountain when I meet one."[18] The prerequisite of innocence may explain why Dillard often identifies stalking and seeing rituals with childhood and childhood games. "Only children keep their eyes open," she writes (104). She describes nature as "like one of those line drawings of a tree that are puzzles for children: Can you find hidden in the leaves a duck, a house, a boy, a bucket, a zebra, and a boot?" (18). The universe is a merry-go-round, and the coot is a child's rubber duck (23, 45). Dillard evokes her own childhood, as well as others', and always in the service of seeing, in all senses, the microcosm of Tinker Creek: "If I seek the senses and skill of children . . . I do so only, solely, and entirely that I might look well at the creek" (104). It is a point made again in the conclusion of *The Living* (1992), a novel set during the turn of the century in Bellingham, Washington. Hugh Honer, who as a child had seen "many people dying, and people dead" and had unwittingly set the fire that killed his brother and sister, is a medical student home for a holiday who recalls pleasant boyhood sensations while walking barefoot in the moonless night along a forest path to a pond where others are swimming. In the darkness, he can see "nothing: no pond, no ocean, no forest, sky, nor any horizon, only unmixed blackness" and yet, in a trancelike state, he takes a rope and swings off a platform over the pond, affirming life through this youthful act:

> As he swung through the air, trembling, he saw the blackness give way below, like a parting of clouds, to a deep patch of stars on the ground. It was the pond, he hoped, the hole in the woods reflecting the sky. He judged the instant and let go; he flung himself loose into the stars. (397)

It is the moment of grace restoring a childlike innocence against a background of horror, confusion, and doubt reminiscent of the spiritual crisis signaled by another child being burned in *Holy the Firm*.

Childhood games coax the Creator from hiding. Dillard al-

ludes to John Knoepfle's poem in which " 'Christ is red rover
. . . and the children are calling / come over come over' " (*PTC*,
209). Longing for God, she compares the "banging" of her will
with a child beating on a door and calling: "Come on out! . . . I
know you're there" (209).

That she seeks to see by entering "the spirit's unself-conscious state" through "pure devotion to any object" is one of
many obvious signs that Annie Dillard is intensely aware of her
own absorption in meditative traditions. Her efforts to see are
rewarded in the numerous mystical moments recorded in *Pilgrim at Tinker Creek*, *Holy the Firm*, and *Teaching a Stone to Talk*.
For instance, one summer evening when she is practicing being
"an unscrupulous observer" of shiners feeding in Tinker Creek

> something broke and something opened. I filled up like a new
> wineskin. I breathed an air like light; I saw a light like water. I
> was the lip of a fountain the creek filled forever; I was ether, the
> leaf in the zephyr; I was flesh-flake, feather, bone . . . (*PTC*,
> 33–34)

Because of such moments, critics have rightly seen in Dillard's mystical experiences parallels with Ralph Waldo Emerson's experiences and views recorded in "Nature." Her observation that "there is [a] kind of seeing that involves a letting go
[and] when I see this way I sway transfixed and emptied" is
justifiably compared with Emerson's famous statement that "I
become a transparent eyeball; I am nothing; I see all; the currents of the Universal Being circulate through me."[19]

Dillard also is Emersonian in preparing herself for vision by
exercising her "Understanding," by disciplining her nature experiences with scientific information and ideas. While she
rightly states "I am no scientist," her essays are packed with
allusions to scientific reading of all sorts. Not surprisingly,
those allusions fall into two dichotomous categories (*PTC*, 12).
One evokes a nature that is the deterministic, the Darwinian
world Krutch outlines in *The Modern Temper*—the insect world
in which a giant water bug sucks out the innards of a frog, "a
monstrous and horrifying thing" that leaves her deeply shaken
(*PTC*, 61). In a more lighthearted moment, she makes the same

point in a chapter about nature's horrors: "Fish gotta swim and bird [sic] gotta fly; insects, it seems, gotta do one horrible thing after another" (65). The other category of scientific allusions focuses on the indeterminant nature described by twentieth-century physics. In the chapter "Stalking," in *Pilgrim at Tinker Creek*, for instance, Dillard has a two-page commentary on Werner Heisenberg's "Principle of Indeterminacy" and quotes, in addition, physicists Sir Arthur Eddington and Sir James Jeans whose views, she notes gleefully, mean that "some physicists now are a bunch of wild-eyed, raving mystics" (206–8). To illustrate, she quotes Eddington's statement that the Principle of Indeterminacy " 'leaves us with no clear distinction between the Natural and the Supernatural' " (207–8).

Critics, especially Gary McIlroy and Margaret Reimer, have pointed out Dillard's responses to science, especially to the Principle of Indeterminacy.[20] Her ritual preparation for seeing, however, has depended upon a broader range of science and science-related reading than they have discussed. Often her reading is specific to phenomena she observes. When she stalks the muskrat, she refers to biologist and expert on muskrats Paul Errington (197). She refers to biologist and science historian Howard Ensign Evans on dragonflies (67), limnologist Robert E. Coker on plankton movement, Rutherford Platt on trees (noting that his *Great American Forest* is "one of the most interesting books ever written"), and so on (97). In Emersonian fashion she "disciplines" her "Understanding" in preparing for visions.

Two writers important in disciplining Dillard's own understanding are Frenchman Henri Fabre (1823–1915) and American Edwin Way Teale (1899–1980), sources for a number of her comments on the horrors of the insect world. In her chapter "The Fixed," in *Pilgrim at Tinker Creek*, which contains some of her most pessimistic and horrific conclusions, Dillard refers frequently to Fabre. She notes that "even a hardened entomologist like J. Henri Fabre confessed to being startled witless every time" a praying mantis strikes its prey, and she quotes a long passage of his describing the macabre mantis mating ritual during which the female gnaws on her "swain" until there is just that "masculine stump" going "on with the business" (56,

59).[21] Edwin Way Teale is the most frequently cited writer in the other dark chapter, "Fecundity," in *Pilgrim at Tinker Creek*, in which nature seems primarily a matter of eating, breeding, and dying: the "universe that suckled us is a monster that does not care if we live or die. . . . It is fixed and blind, programmed to kill" (180). She illustrates this grim, amoral natural world with examples drawn from Teale's *Strange Lives of Familiar Insects*, which is, she exclaims, a "book I couldn't live without" (171).

Although she draws upon Fabre's and Teale's writings to underscore a deterministic, amoral, natural world that may be "the brainchild of a deranged manic-depressive with unlimited capital," these writers achieved their fame as popularizers of science by maintaining optimistic spiritual outlooks (*PTC*, 67). Fabre never accepted Darwinian evolutionary theory and remained a devout Roman Catholic. A humble French provincial, not accepted by the academy until very late in life, Fabre was less the laboratory scientist in white lab coat than a living example of the persona familiar to the nature essay in general and to Annie Dillard's essay in particular—the amateur who is faithful to his local environment and who experiences awe and wonder in nature's small moments. Teale, who admired Fabre and introduced the English translation of his collected essays, is also optimistic despite his chronicles of the violent and grotesque insect world.[22] In *Speaking for Nature*, Paul Brooks describes Teale as one of the finest "literary naturalists" since Thoreau, who with others has "opened the eyes of millions of readers . . . to a widespread feeling of kinship with the other forms of life with which we share the earth" (xiv). Teale's ability to evoke this kinship literarily was a major reason Rachel Carson admired him and sought his advice. From his *Strange Lives of Familiar Insects* to his widely read and well-regarded books on the American seasons, Teale's works reflect the affirmation and joy characteristic of American nature writers and, in fact, of one side of Annie Dillard's dialectical view. Certainly, the two men offered her more than scientific information even as she disciplined herself to see more fully.

In her intellectual preparations for reaching a state of innocence followed by mystical insight, Dillard focuses her atten-

tion on reading as much as on natural objects. The reading is
diverse: theology and other religious matters (Martin Buber,
Thomas Merton, Julia[n] of Norwich, the Koran); art (Leonardo
da Vinci, Van Gogh, Brueghel, El Greco); adventure (Lewis and
Clark, Thor Heyerdahl, the Franklin polar expedition); and literature (Thoreau, Coleridge, Blake, Goethe, Eliot). A full accounting of the interplay between Dillard's reading and her responses to nature is impractical here, but I must discuss one
crucial intellectual source—the philosopher Heraclitus, whom
Dillard quotes and associates with views close to those of quan-
tum physics, that " 'nature is wont to hide herself' " (*PTC*,
205). Moreover, his perspective is akin to her dialectical vision.
She opens *Pilgrim at Tinker Creek* with the following epigraph
from Heraclitus:

> It ever was, and is, and shall be,
> ever-living Fire, in measures being
> kindled and in measures going out.

Heraclitus was the philosopher of opposites. But the opposites have underlying connections; for instance, good and evil
define one another. The same is true for all natural events:
while seen and described in terms of opposites, there is an underlying interrelatedness, a hidden connection, of which fire is
the physical embodiment.[23] The epigraph in *Pilgrim* and the
pervasive fire imagery in *Holy the Firm* signify that the intellectual aspects of her meditations prepare her for a sense of wonder no less than for horrific vision. As a result, she sees not
only the dead frog but also the "tree with the lights in it . . .
transfigured, each cell buzzing with flame" (*PTC*, 35). The
flaming tree is a vision that, as Heraclitus would have pre-
dicted, comes and goes. It is a vision she lives for. In that moment her spirit's aspirations and her own reality are melded. In
Holy the Firm, the fire is the fire that attracts the moth to destruction and that disfigures Julie; but it is also the light that
comes into Dillard's spirit and appears on her face, as onto the
face of every artist, which, "like a seraph's" face, lights "the
kingdom of God for the people to see" (77). Heraclitus's imagery of eternally waxing and waning fire is the perfect metaphor

for her thematic dualities of evil and good, grotesque and beautiful, and repulsive and awesome, all of which co-exist in God's nature.

At times, however, her ritual stalking and ritual preparations to see are undercut by the grotesque in nature. Reading, in particular, is not a sufficient stay against confusion. Dillard discovers that she can become lost in the "labyrinthine tracks of the mind" when she most needs to live in the senses (*PTC*, 88). "So long as I stay in my thoughts . . . my foot slides" and "I fall," she writes, echoing the text for Jonathan Edwards's *Sinners in the Hands of an Angry God* (88). For example, in *Teaching a Stone to Talk* Dillard encounters a Guernsey cow during one of her rambles and is shocked to find that it is dead. The cow's insides are gone, "her udder and belly . . . open and empty." Horrified, Dillard sees that the cow's legs had broken when a limestone sinkhole had suddenly opened under her weight (168). Dillard is shocked and disoriented, fearing that the ground will open beneath her and she will fall unchecked (168). The passage echoes the creekside frog episode in *Pilgrim at Tinker Creek*, in which the alternative to falling, to terror, and to doubt is to dance (*PTC*, 88). Ritual dance, literal or imagined, allows Dillard to quiet morbid intellectualizing, to enter the natural world directly, and to offer praise despite the threat of meaninglessness. Dance is her least mentioned ritual, but it is crucial for keeping her spiritual balance.

In *Pilgrim at Tinker Creek* imagery of falling and dancing combine as she seeks signs of hope but fears that the monstrous may prevail. Near the book's end, she describes herself as a "sojourner seeking signs" and remembers that Isak Dinesen, brokenhearted, had stepped into the Kenyan morning seeking a sign and had witnessed a rooster tear from its root a chameleon's tongue–the unwelcome sign again of pervasive cruelty. But Dillard's thoughts and feelings about that shocking moment in Dinesen's experience and about cruelty in nature are altered; she is once again "transfigured" as a maple key twirls down toward her on the wind. She becomes aware of that other "wind of the spirit" and thinks, "If I am a maple leaf falling, at least I can twirl" (275–76). Similarly, in concluding "Sojourner" in *Teaching a Stone to Talk*, Dillard turns from "thoughts of despair" about the purposelessness she senses everywhere to thoughts of beauty, just as Edward Abbey's antidote to despair is to think about "the beauty of art and nature and life, and the love which that beauty inspires" (*JH*, 57). Dillard invites us, just as Abbey might, "with as much spirit as we can muster, [to] go out with a buck and wing" (152). That said, she envisions nature joining in: "the consort of musicians strikes up, and we in the chorus stir and move and start twirling our hats. A mangrove island turns drift to dance . . . rocking over the salt sea at random, rocking day and night and round the sun, rocking round the sun and out toward east of Hercules" (152). Moreover, as she has with stalking and seeing, Dillard locates the dance ritual within the tradition of Judeo-Christian ritual and mysticism. She recalls that King David "leaped and danced naked before the ark of the Lord in a barren desert," a model for herself in the face of spiritual emptiness, and a reminder to us, she says, to "make connections; let rip; and dance whenever you can" (97–98). She is dancing, significantly, as *A Pilgrim at Tinker Creek* ends: "I go my way and my left foot says 'Glory,' and my right foot says 'Amen' in and out of Shadow Creek, upstream and down, exultant, in a daze, dancing to the two silver trumpets of praise" (279).

There are powerful moments in *Pilgrim at Tinker Creek* when Annie Dillard, performing her stalking, seeing, and dancing rituals has the sudden insight that not only is she stalking, she is being stalked; not only is she seeing but she is being seen; not only is she dancing but music is being played for her. On the dark side, God is a stalker-hunter, a destroyer, who is the ultimate " 'archer in cover' " whose arrows bring fear and mortality (91). Being seen, though, is joyful. In the central mystical moment of the book when Dillard is taken unaware by the "tree with the lights in it," she exclaims that "it was less like seeing than like being for the first time seen, knocked breathless by a powerful glance" (35). We do not need to be told who has seen her; the agent of the dance is more than nature. When Dillard spins in her imagination through the universe in order to retard her "sweeping fall," "Someone" pipes as "we are dancing a tarantella until the sweat pours" (23).

Having divined that she is stalked, seen as well as seeing, a dancer to "Someone's" tune, she concludes that she "cannot ask for more than to be so wholly acted upon," even if by a plague of locusts, since she would willingly pay the price in discomfort to be "rapt and enwrapped" in the "real world" (226). Her imagery of being acted upon climaxes as the book ends in passages about ritual sacrifice which, again, combine her personal vision with the Judeo-Christian.

As she debates whether corruption and beauty are equal in creation and concludes that corruption is not "beauty's very heart," she describes herself as "a sacrifice bound with cords to the horns of the world's rock altar." There she takes a deep breath and opens her eyes, seeing "worms in the horn of the altar," as "a sense of the real exults me; the cords loose; I walk on my way" (248). In this mystical moment, she finds freedom in accepting the fallen world. But she needs to go beyond supplication and acceptances to praise, from "please" to "thank you." And she does. The last two chapters of *Pilgrim at Tinker Creek* focus on sacrificial rituals which Dillard must know are in the Judeo-Christian tradition, rituals of purification and thanksgiving rather than merely propitiating the gods. She concentrates on an ancient Israelite ritual, "the wave breast of thanksgiving" which is, significantly, considering Dillard's joy in being seen, "a catching [of] God's eye" (266). The priest dresses in clean linen, comes to the altar, and is given a consecrated breastbone of a ritually slain ram, which he waves as an offering to the Lord. She knows the ritual of thanksgiving is efficacious, and she ends discussion with a phrase from Catholic liturgy: "Thanks be to God" (266). A second part to the ritual, however, she calls upon to acknowledge her ongoing problem with the cruel, horrible, and monstrous in nature. After the priest waves the breastbone, he "heaves" the ram's shoulder bone. Dillard interprets this to mean that after catching God's eye, one can "speak up for the creation," can protest cruelty and waste in the natural world. "Could I heave a little shred of frog shoulder at the Lord?" she muses, remembering, of course, the frog's death she had witnessed at creekside. She frequently understands, though, that the "wave" to capture God's glance and the "heave" to lodge protest are both necessary for a unified ritual: "both meant a wide-eyed and keen-eyed thanks"; neither was whole without the other (279).

As one stalking and being stalked, seeing and being seen, dancing to Someone's tune, performing rituals of sacrifice, and as victim of the sacrifice, Dillard places herself in a mystical relationship with both a nature and a God who are at once both concealed and revealed. She concludes with prayers of affirmation, no matter how bleak the moment's reality. In *Teaching a Stone to Talk*, she notes that Americans "as a people have moved from pantheism to pan-atheism" (69). We have desacralized nature, she says, and God no longer speaks from the whirlwind. Until "God changes his mind, until the pagan gods slip back to their hilltop groves, or until we can teach a stone to talk, all we can do with the whole inhuman array is watch it" (72). "We are here to witness . . . The silence is all there is." Nevertheless, she concludes with an exhortation to prayer: "you take a step in the right direction to pray to this silence . . . Pray without ceasing" (72, 76).

The remarkable conclusion to *Holy the Firm* is, in effect, an extended, unceasing prayer that does reveal the God beyond nature who is linked with it by "holy the firm." Here the book's major thematic and artistic elements coalesce. The images of the burning moth, Julie the burned child, and Annie Dillard herself are intertwined with Puget Sound's "islands on fire" and seraphs' and the artist's faces that "can sing only the first 'Holy' before the intensity of their love ignites them again and dissolves them again, perpetually, into flames."[24] Dillard is the artist-nun, aflame with holiness; Dillard's book-prayer is "lighting the kingdom of God for the people to see."[25]

If Dillard's Christian desire to light up the "kingdom of God" sets her apart from other nature writers, it is only to a matter of degree. All non-Christian writers I have mentioned, and there are others, are fascinated with the relationships between nature, human consciousness, and "mystery." Troubled by the combined intellectual and spiritual consequences of Newtonian and Cartesian thought, which separated spirit and matter and placed nature beneath humans in importance; troubled by nonteleological Darwinian natural selection, and by technological assaults on the natural environment, twentieth-century nature writers have explored alternative views. Committed to science as guide, writers as diverse as Joseph Wood Krutch, Edward Abbey, Gary Snyder, Loren Eiseley, Peter Matthiessen, Barry Lopez, and Ann Zwinger have, nevertheless, kept as their first loyalty and touchstone direct, experiential encounters with nature. All report aesthetic and spiritual rewards for doing so. In Dillard's essays, the same persona speaks to us as from the works of other nature writers — the solitary figure in nature, moved to philosophical speculation and, finally, moved to awe and wonder, to self-forgetting, and to an affirmation of realities that resist modern and contemporary threats of hopelessness and despair.

Despite such affinities, Annie Dillard has a special voice that speaks of balancing tensions between fear and hope, horror and celebration, through rituals of stalking, seeing, and dancing. In such rituals, she not only awakens to mystery in nature but to mystery beyond nature. Her Christian preoccupations and ritual practice culminate in prayer without cessation; I "resound," she writes, "like a beaten bell" (*PTC*, 13).

6
Gary Snyder: Posthumanist

Pull down thy vanity, I say pull down. Learn of the green world what
can be thy place.
—Ezra Pound (1972)

Place is the only reality, the true core of the universal.
—William Carlos Williams (1958)

In response to a friendly note from Pulitzer Prize-winning poet,
essayist, and environmental activist Gary Snyder, a high-
spirited Edward Abbey wrote: " 'Dear Gary, I admire your
work too, except for all that Zen and Hindu bullshit' " (AR,
xvi). Snyder responded with a good-spirited, open letter, commenting upon misunderstood aspects of Buddhism and invit-
ing Abbey to join him in the comradeship of environmental activism and a walk together along "some ridge or canyon" (RM,
145). They do have common environmental and social concerns, as Snyder's letter points out. Moreover, Gary Snyder
and Ed Abbey share activist friends, such as deep ecologist
George Sessions and Earth First!'s Dave Foreman. The groups
of activist comrades Snyder welcomes to the cause in his letter
are identical to those Abbey lists in his "Earth First! Rendezvous" chapter in *Hayduke Lives!*: "I welcome," Snyder writes,
"neo-shamanists, mother-goddess worshipers, neo-pagans,
and whatever else to the scene if that helps them get the energy
to go to work against the industrial civilization. Even Marxists!"
(RM, 144).

Gary Snyder is one of America's singular voices raised in
defense of nature and against industrial civilization. Born in
San Francisco of working-class parents in 1930, Snyder spent
his school years in Washington, Oregon, and California, taking
a dual degree in anthropology and literature at Reed College in

109

1951 and studying linguistics and Oriental languages in graduate school before spending several years in Japan as a student of Zen Buddhism. His education, of course, was more than formal. He has written that when he was young, he had "an immediate, intuitive, deep sympathy with the natural world which was not taught me by anyone. In that sense, nature is my 'guru' " (*RW*, 92). At various times in his earlier years, he worked in the Pacific Northwest wilderness as a member of a trail crew, as a fire lookout in the Cascades, and as a logger for the Warm Springs Lumber Company (*PW*, 68). The lessons he learned from his guru are those learned by Aldo Leopold, Joseph Wood Krutch, and so many others in the tradition of nature writing and environmental activism: "I have had a very moving, profound perception a few times that everything was alive . . . and that on one level there is no hierarchy of qualities in life—that the life of a stone or a weed is as completely beautiful and authentic, wise and valuable as the life of, say, an Einstein" (*RW*, 17). Sounding very much like Krutch, Snyder has concluded that "we're a part of everything" (*RW*, 79).

Ecological concepts and language permeate Snyder's vision. He makes radical extensions of Aldo Leopold's antihierarchical, biocentric perspective, identifying his own position as "posthumanist." In his most recent collection of essays, *The Practice of the Wild* (1990), Snyder defines the term:

> The "post" in the term *posthumanism* is on account of the word *human*. The dialogue to open next would be among all beings, towards a rhetoric of ecological relationships. This is not to put down the human: the "proper study of mankind" *is* what it means to be human. It's not enough to be shown in school that we are kin to all the rest: we have to feel it all the way through. Then we can also be uniquely "human" with no sense of special privilege. (68)

A "rhetoric of ecological relationships" is the key to Snyder's voice raised in defense of nature, society, and art. This posthumanist, ecological vision, encompassing such vast and complex subjects, is rooted in Snyder's attention to the local and particular—to place. Ideally, place, in the here-and-now, is where nature, social community, and spiritual achievement are brought into balance with one another. For Snyder, ecological relationships are found not only in nature but, analogously, in relations among people in communities. Even more broadly, Snyder uses a "rhetoric of ecological relationship" to outline an ecological vision in which nature, society, and spirit are interdependent: what happens in nature has social and spiritual consequences; what happens politically and economically has natural and spiritual consequences; and what happens spiritually has social and natural consequences. Gary Snyder's life-long interest in place creates a focus for this ecological vision that intermingles ecological language and concept with anthropology and art.

Snyder does not accept conventional political descriptions and divisions into places, such as "Northern California." He writes in the introductory note to his best-known volume of poems and essays, *Turtle Island* (1974), that "The 'U. S. A.,' and its states and counties are arbitrary and inaccurate impositions on what is really here." "Turtle Island" is a better "address" because it is the Indian name for North America linked to "creation myths of people living here for millennia"; and such a name allows us to "see ourselves more accurately on this continent of watersheds and life-communities—plant zones, physiographic provinces, culture areas; following natural boundaries" (*TI*, unpaginated). His own Northern California homestead address as it has appeared in print does not have a post office zip code. It is "Shasta Nation, Turtle Island, Third Planet out from the Sun," or more ecologically it is "Watershed: west slope of the northern Sierra Nevada, south slope of the east-west running ridge above the south fork, at the level of Black oak mixed with Ponderosa pine."[1] He has *re*-inhabited this place because it was originally inhabited by Native Americans and later logged and burned by turn-of-the-century entrepreneurs.

The most widely respected and often quoted geographers, such as Yi-fu Tuan, Edward Ralph, and James Houston, have convinced other geographers what is common sense for most of us—that mere space is not place. Houston, for instance, states:

> Space . . . has no meaning other than a mathematic one . . . Place, on the other hand, has a human context: space with historical associations where vows are made; encounters and obligations, met; commitments fulfilled; limits recognized. Place implies belonging. It establishes identity. It defines vocation. It envisions destiny. Place is filled with memories of life that provide roots and give direction.[2]

Gary Snyder would agree with these humanist geographers as far as they go, but he argues for a yet more encompassing humanism ("posthumanism") that would "include the non-human"—plant life, animals, even mountain ranges, as well as human beings (*TI*, 107–08).

This not-so-common-sensical viewpoint is a conceptual foundation for figures as different as Aldo Leopold and Edward Abbey, as well as for contemporary environmental activists. The vows made, obligations met, commitments fulfilled, limits recognized, and roots established and honored occur ideally in a human community that is integrated with nature. The problem has been, of course, that vows and commitments have been broken, limits ignored, and roots severed. In our century a body of writing has emerged about dis-placement and placelessness—the loss of identity, of cultural memory, of disrupted connections between people and the land. Its philosopher is Martin Heidegger and its most powerful symbolic express is T. S. Eliot's "The Wasteland." Gary Snyder has written in anger and sorrow about loss of place in his earliest poems and essays in *Myths & Texts* (1960) and *Earth House Hold* (1969); in the Pulitzer Prize–winning *Turtle Island* (1974); the interviews and essays in *The Real Work* (1980); recent poetry in *Axe Handles* (1983), *Left Out in the Rain* (1986), and *No Nature* (1992); and the most recent essays in *The Practice of the Wild* (1990). The loss is a political and spiritual concern, and he has pointed to underlying causes in the Judeo-Christian tradition, industrial capitalism, and in greed, arrogance, and ignorance. Anger and sorrow permeate the following poem (no. 14) from the "Logging" section of *Myths & Texts*:

> The groves are down
>   cut down
> Groves of Ahab, of Cybele
> Pine trees, knobbed twigs
>   thick cone and seed
>   Cybele's tree this, sacred in groves
> Pine of Seami, cedar of Haida
> Cut down by the prophets of Israel
>   the fairies of Athens
>   the thugs of Rome
>   both ancient and modern;
> Cut down to make room for the suburbs
> Bulldozed by Luther and Weyerhaeuser
> Crosscut and chainsaw
>   squareheads and finns
>   high-lead and cat-skidding
> Trees down
> Creeks choked, trout killed, roads.
>
> Sawmill temples of Jehovah.
> Squat black burners 100 feet high
> Sending the smoke of our burnt
> Live sap and leaf
> To his eager nose.

There can be no escaping the land's ruination. For Americans who think they can escape the reality of landscape ravaged and culture dehumanized by finding their Walden Pond or "lighting out for the territory" Snyder warns:

> There is no place to flee to in the U. S. There is no "country" that you can go and lay back in. There is no quiet place in the woods . . . The surveyors are there with their orange plastic tape, the bulldozers are down the road warming up their engines, the real estate developers have got it all on the wall with pins in it, the county supervisors are in the back room drinking coffee with the real estate subdividers . . . and the forest service is just about to let out a big logging contract to some company. (*RW*, 118)

Gary Snyder is not simply, however, another American Jeremiah or poet of placelessness and dis-placement. He is, rather, the most articulate champion for the positive vision of "re-inhabiting." In an essay entitled "Re-Inhabitation," he refers to

> the tiny number of persons who come out of the industrial societies . . . and then start to turn back to the land, to place. This comes for some with the rational and scientific realization of inter-connectedness, and planetary limits. But the actual demands of a life committed to place . . . are so physically and intellectually intense, that it is a moral and spiritual choice as well. (*OW*, 65).

To re-inhabit a place, one must have an ecological perspective that affirms interconnectedness and acknowledges limits, a perspective that extends beyond the intellectual to an ethical and spiritual vision. Beyond anger and sorrow, Snyder has faith that cultures will eventually emerge from people who share commitments to places and who honor their roots.

Snyder's ideas are reflected by Kirkpatrick Sale in *Dwellers in the Land: The Bioregional Vision* (1985). "To become dwellers in the land . . . the crucial and perhaps only and all-encompassing task is to understand '*place*' " (42). Or, as Snyder writes in a discussion of bioregionalism in "The Place, the Region, and the Commons": "Our relation to the natural world takes place in a *place*, and it must be grounded in information and experience" (*PW*, 39). We must begin by "knowing the land" or, as Snyder exhorts us in the poem "For the Children," we must "*learn the flowers*" (*TI*, 86). A measure of alienation, he notes, is that many "contemporary Americans don't even *know* that they don't 'know the plants' " (*PW*, 39). Poets, of course, should know "the names of trees and flowers and weeds."[3] To the rest of us he says, "You should really know what the complete natural world of your region is and know what all its interactions are and how you are interacting with it yourself. This is just part of the work of becoming who you are, where you are" (*RW*, 16).

Knowing the land, for Snyder, must be based in experience. One must know the land with "one's body, commitment, time, labor, walking" (*RW*, 23). For him, as for Annie Dillard, walking is a form of spiritual practice, of meditation. It is "the great adventure, the first meditation, a practice of heartiness and soul primary to humankind. Walking is the exact balance of spirit and humility." (*PW*, 18). It puts one in touch with the most physical ("out walking one notices where there is food"); reminds us of "interdependence, interconnection," the essential truth of ecology; and leads us while on the literal trail along a spiritual path (*PW*, 18, 144).

Above and beyond the directly experiential encounter with nature, with the manzanita plants, flickers, deer, and mountain ridges that fill Snyder's poetry, is intellectual knowledge of the land. While from an early age in the Pacific Northwest Snyder had an "immediate, intuitive, deep sympathy with the natural world," he emphasizes the importance of understanding nature scientifically. To entering university students, he recommends emphatically that they study biology (*RW*, 92). His own study of ecological concepts is apparent throughout his writing. *Earth House Hold*'s title refers to the literal meaning of "ecology"; and the *Axe Handles* collection of poems is divided into three sections, each with a title drawn from ecological language and speculation—"Loops," "Nets," and "Little Songs for Gaia." The body of Snyder's writing is a remarkable collection of poems and essays in which the ecological sciences are touchstones for his nonscientific views and artistic practice, as well as his understanding of natural processes and the significance of place.

A reading of his entire work reveals the poet-essayist's indebtedness to a handful of distinguished and intriguing biologists and biological works for his intellectual understanding of nature's operations. They are for him what William Morton Wheeler was for Joseph Wood Krutch and Henri Fabre and Edwin Way Teale were for Annie Dillard. They scientifically confirm his experiences in nature. Chief among them is Eugene Odum, described by a reviewer of his influential *Fundamentals of Ecology* (1971) as "the world's foremost ecologist."[4] Snyder also frequently alludes to Eugene Odum's brother and collaborator, Howard T. Odum, whose provocative *Environment, Power and Society* (1971) made an impact on Snyder with both its information about nature and its speculations about politics and religion. A third ecologist who deeply impressed the poet is the Spanish scientist Ramon Margalef, whose *Perspectives in Ecological Theory* (1968) is frequently mentioned by Snyder and the Odum brothers.[5] These three ecologists form a special group of distinguished scientists who combine the discussion of basic ecological concepts with a more special focus on energy flow in ecosystems. The major concepts Snyder uses from them are the food chain and succession—concepts formulated during the 1930s and 1940s—as well as contemporary concepts such as the biology of loops and networks.

Eugene Odum explains the concept of food chain as "the transfer of food energy from the source in plants through a series of organisms with repeated states of eating and being eaten."[6] Snyder elaborates poetically and wittily upon sharing physical and emotional energy through eating and being eaten in one of his best-known poems, "The Song of Taste," in which "eating the living germs of grasses / Eating the ova of large birds," culminates with acts of love and promises of fecundity:

> Eating each other's seed
> eating
> ah, each other
>
> Kissing the lover in the mouth of bread:
> lip to lip.[7]

A second generally known and fundamental ecological principle Snyder often refers to is succession. Snyder cites Eugene Odum and Margalef in stating his understanding that essentially in any ecosystem over time there is a pattern of change from initial instability and simplicity to a mature "climax state" of optimum stability and maximum diversity (1977).[8] It is a lesson Aldo Leopold had taught in *A Sand County Almanac*—food chains constitute an energy circuit for the biotic pyramid, and the evolutionary pattern is toward a diverse and stable biota (253). The Odum brothers acknowledge their indebtedness to Margalef for their special understanding of the principle: Margalef discusses this process in terms of energy transfer and as a "process of accumulating information."[9] There is a large use of energy in early states of succession which is "the cost of accumulating information."[10] A stable ecosystem in later stages of succession has "learned" about changes in the environment and can accept new information with less change and energy. Biomass is the bearer of that information, and there is, then, a "wisdom" in a mature ecosystem. Or, as Snyder paraphrases Eugene Odum, himself paraphrasing Margalef:

> Life biomass . . . is stored information; living matter is stored information in the cells and in the genes. . . . There is more information of a higher order of sophistication and complexity stored in a few square yards of forest than there is in all the libraries of mankind. (*TI*, 107)

Nature is text. Since a "text is information stored through time," the "stratigraphy of rocks, layers of pollen in a swamp, the outward expanding circles in the trunk of a tree, can be seen as texts" (*PW*, 66).

Mistreated ecosystems become unstable because that wisdom is lost. To minimize instability and loss, there are "loop circuits," as Howard T. Odum calls them. In a feedback loop the recipient of energy "rewards its source by passing necessary materials back to it."[11] Odum's example is of animals returning minerals to the soil which allow plants to grow and in turn feed the animal. Snyder mentions that he learned from Eugene Odum and Margalef about succession and that in a climax state "half of the energy that flows in the system does not come from annual growth, it comes from the recycling of dead growth"; in fact, efficient recycling is a mark of a mature system (*RW*, 115, 116). That there is poetic value for Snyder in such a feedback loop is apparent in his poem "Old Rotting Tree Trunk Down":

> If "meditation on decay and rot cures lust"
> I'm hopeless:
> I delight in thought of fungus,
> beetle larvae, stains
>   that suck the life still
>   from your old insides, . . .

Corruption, decay, the sticky turnover—
Death into more of the
Life-death same,

A quick life:
and the long slow
feeding that follows—
the woodpecker's cry.[12]

Snyder values these biological-ecological views not only as accounts of natural phenomena, but also for their social, political, and cultural implications. Eugene Odum emphasizes in his influential textbook that "ecology has grown from a division of biological science to a major interdisciplinary science that links together the biological, physical, and social sciences."[13] All these ecologists are concerned with social issues ranging from the predictable conservationists' and environmentalists' topics of pollution and resource depletion to unorthodox topics. That is especially true of Howard T. Odum, who argues that "energy language" can be used to "consider the pressing problems of survival in our time" and that "energy analysis can help answer many of the questions of economics, law, and religion, already stated in other languages."[14] Aldo Leopold a generation before had established the practice of using the ecological language of "community" to include humans and "the land" among the pressing conservation problems. Snyder, too, is willing to make direct connections between scientific language and nonscientific. When "ecologists talk about ecology of oak communities," Snyder writes, we should understand that "they are communities," that oak and human communities "share attributes" (*TI*, 108). He argues, as did Leopold, that we accept as "citizens" in a broadened sense of political community the "non-human"—plants, animals, and "a variety of wild life" (107–8).

Snyder applies the concept and language of succession to environmental history and social change. In *The Real Work* he observes, "Certain human societies have demonstrated the capacity to become mature in the same way" as natural systems, to reach a "climax state." They are populated by "people of place." The communities are stable and foster diversity. Ironically, the "only societies that are mature," Snyder concludes, "are primitive societies" (116). Contemporary industrial nations are highly unstable, wasteful "monocultures" (116–17). It is an idea he acknowledges as Eugene Odum's: "[I]n Dr. Eugene Odum's terms, what we call civilization is an early succession phase; immature, monoculture system. What we call the primitive is a mature system with deep capacities for stability and protection built into it" (*OW*, 29).

Consequently, Gary Snyder's second injunction for reinhabiting place after "know the flowers" through experience, information, and scientific concept is to "know the lore." Knowing the lore entails discovering how earlier communities lived in that place, not so we can imitate those people literally but to learn from them wisdom we have lost. To recover wisdom is so important that the other subject, after biology, that Snyder encourages college students to study above all else is anthropology: "Anthropology," he says, "is probably the most intellectually exciting field in the universities" (*RW*, 58). He himself wrote an undergraduate thesis, later published, about a Haida Indian myth, and certainly Native American lore is central to much of his finest poetry–especially in *Myths & Texts*.[15]

In *The Real Work* Snyder explains his approach in seeking to define the lore of his own Northern California region. Initially he found it useful to superimpose a map that showed California locations of the "original Indian culture groups and tribes (culture areas)" on other maps that located watersheds and other ecological features (24). He also recommends discarding the European name of a place (as he did in substituting "Turtle Island" for North America) (69). It can be done anywhere in America: "Learn about Cincinnati . . . get rid of the name *Cincinnati* . . . because after all it's the Ohio River Valley, really, that you're looking at. And *Ohio* means *beautiful* in [the] Shawnee [language]. And there you go, you start going back and connecting with all those loops" (59). Links will be forged between past and present. Even city dwellers will learn about links to natural settings and earlier peoples. Cities in most cases were "tribal marketplaces" at the "mouths of rivers, or at fords

on rivers—hence *Oxford* University." They may find that their
city was the goal of religious pilgrimage to a sacred place, such
as Jerusalem (69–70).

Snyder agrees with anthropologist Stanley Diamond that
" 'the sickness of civilization consists in its failure to incorporate (and only then) to move beyond the limits of the primitive.' "[16] To Snyder, contemporary social and political lessons
can be drawn from knowledge of the practices of primitive "in-
habitory people":

1. We can have neighborhoods and communities "strong in
their sense of place, proud and aware of local and special qualities" (*RW*, 161).

2. Environmental responsibility comes from people who
work and live together in their place (161). This will help contemporary environmentalism advance. Quoting bioregionalist
Peter Nabokov, Snyder reports that "good-hearted environmentalists can turn their back on a save-the-wilderness project
when it gets too tiresome and return to a city home. But inhab-
itory people will 'fight for their lives like they've been jumped
in an alley.' "[17]

3. "Rootedness" will move people to make changes, even
revolutionary ones, in the ways they organize their politics and
economies. They will move toward decentralized, steady-state
economies as farming practices and business practices become
harmonious with ecological circumstances. The Pueblo Indian
societies, like other primitive groups, "practiced a kind of ultimate democracy" in which "plants and animals are also people
. . . and given a place and a voice" in politics through ritual and
dance (*TI*, 104).

The overarching approach for establishing new contemporary social, political, and economic realities is to integrate and
absorb "primitive . . . models of . . . nature related cultures"
with the "most imaginative extensions of science." Where the
"two vectors cross," we should "build a community" (*TI*, 102).

The most important benefits of such a place can be spiritual. One of the lessons learned from studying the "lore" is
how primitives sacralized place by uniting wild nature and culture through religious belief and spiritual practice. Although
nineteenth-century Romantics resacralized wilderness, Snyder

argues that "very old place centered cultures" go beyond a romantic "vague sense of the sacred" to speak to us about "sacred groves, sacred land" within a "context of genuine belief and practice" (*PW*, 80).

In many essays, from "Poetry and the Primitive" in *Earth House Hold* to "Good, Wild, Sacred" in *The Practice of the Wild*, Gary Snyder has repeatedly outlined his credo that sacred places "take us (not only human beings) out of our little selves into the whole mountains-and-rivers mandala universe" (*PW*, 93). To have a true sense of place is to live in the sacred. Native American traditions, as well as the Buddhist traditions Snyder follows, teach us how to get out of our "little selves." Native Americans and Buddhists share in the wisdom traditions by having inherently ecological understandings of the interdependencies and equality of all living and nonliving "citizens" of nature. These ancient traditions should combine with modern ecological science, which, Snyder concludes, has been

> laying out (implicitly) a spiritual dimension. We must find our way to seeing the mineral cycles, the water cycles, air cycles, nutrient cycles, as sacramental—and we must incorporate that insight into our own personal spiritual quest and integrate it with all the wisdom teachings we have received from the . . . past. (*OW*, 63)

According to Native American and Buddhist traditions, all things express Original Mind—that state of awareness that is free from presuppositions and untarnished by narrow, sectarian religious education. Not only humans express it, but animals, plants, and even rocks and the earth. Through ritual story and dance, a group's shaman, whether Indian Medicine man or Buddhist teacher, has access to Original Mind. Through community rituals that the shaman leads, everyone shares life in a sacralized natural and social community. Through story, for example, the contents of external wilderness, its wild creatures, and of internal wilderness, the unconscious, are brought into culture and reconciled. A sense of this can be gotten from Snyder's poem "this poem is for bear." It embraces the mysteries of the animal/human relationship (bear/girl) and wild/

domestic interdependency in hunting the bear for food. The narrative is a Native American story about a girl who married a bear as well as a ritual chant that prepares the hunter spiritually so that the bear will choose death in order to feed him:

> "As for me I am a child of the god of the mountains."

> A bear down under the cliff.
> She is eating huckleberries.
> They are ripe now
> Soon it will snow, and she
> Or maybe he, will crawl into a hole
> And sleep. . . .

> The others had all gone down
> From the blackberry brambles, but one girl
> Spilled her basket, and was picking up her
> Berries in the dark.
> A tall man stood in the shadow, took her arm,
> Led her to his home. He was a bear.
> In a house under the mountain
> She gave birth to slick dark children
> With sharp teeth, and lived in the hollow
> Mountain many years.
>   snare a bear: call him out:
> honey-eater
> forest apple
> light-foot
> Old man in the fur coat, Bear! come out!
> Die of your own choice! . . .[18]

Snyder's interest in shamanism is long standing— beginning as early as his undergraduate thesis, which employs his reading of Joseph Campbell's studies of myth and Carl Jung's interpretation of archetypes to discuss the shaman's trance and dream journey as a way to make conscious and public the unconscious knowledge of his primitive community's members.[19] And shamanism often appears in the essays and interviews collected in *The Real Work*. Snyder is fascinated with the essential identity between the shaman and the poet. Poems at their best, be believes, come from Original Mind (*RW*, 79). In words that should be applied to Snyder himself, he writes that the shaman-poet is "simply the man whose mind reaches easily out into all manners of shapes and other lives, and gives song to dreams."[20] He is a voice for the voiceless citizens of wild — the "creeping people, and the standing people, and the flying people, and the swimming people" (*TI*, 108). The utter simplicity of such a conception and knowledge is caught in poems such as "The Flickers" in the "Little Songs for Gaia" section of *Axe Handles*, a volume of poetry whose setting is Snyder's place in the Sierra foothills. The shaman-poet's voice brings together the two guises of Indian Medicine Man and Buddhist teacher:

THE FLICKERS

sharp clear call

THIS!

THIS!

THIS!

in the cool pine breeze

The flicker in the pine woods is a familiar bird to whom the shaman-poet gives voice. Its call is both its own brought to us by the medicine man and, according to Buddhist literary and religious tradition, an invitation to the noumenal world. If we are patient, Snyder writes in another context, the sacred will reveal itself in "the cry of the Flicker" (*PW*, 96).

What the shaman was to primitive culture, the poet and other artists are to contemporary reinhabited space. Beyond the ecological and economical benefits of reinhabiting place and living according to a bioregional ethic are spiritual benefits of place which poets voice. By reinhabiting place through knowing the land and its lore, we can overcome alienation as people and "learn that community is of spiritual benefit and of health for everyone, that ongoing working relationships and shared concerns, music, poetry, and stories all evolve into the shared practice of a set of values, visions, and quests. That's what the spiritual path really is" (*RW*, 141).

Snyder's most extended discussion of the function of poetry in reinhabited places appears in "Poetry, Community & Climax" (*RW*, 159–74), which is a revision and extension of ideas originally in the chapter "Poetry and the Primitive: Notes on Poetry as an Ecological Survival Technique" in *Earth House Hold*. He gives a recent history of public poetry in the United States since the 1950s, when Allen Ginsberg and others began poetry readings that inspired countless more. Snyder argues that people who gather for readings create a community that is more than literary (for example, the counter-culture). Among the poets who read, Snyder identifies the "home-growers." These poets

> live in a place with some intention of staying there—and begin to find their poetry playing a useful role in the daily life of the neighborhood. Poetry as a tool, a net or trap to catch and present; a sharp edge; a medicine, or the little awl that unties knots. (*RW*, 167)

Usually unknown outside their communities, these poets express an alternative to the culture manufactured by television and newspapers. This kind of decentralized culture "is as important to our long-range ecological and social health," Snyder claims, "as the decentralization of agriculture, production, energy, and government" (169). Such poets and their poems speak "to what is happening *here*." On one hand, they bring simple pleasure. Snyder delights in the "pleasure in the eyes of the audience when a local tree, a local river or mountain, comes swirling forth as part of proto-epic or myth" (168). On the other hand, the poets "shine a little ray of myth on things; memory turning to legend" (168). Given his own commitment to poetry, to place, to *here*, it is not surprising that Snyder regards as equal honors invitations to read at the United States Library of Congress and at the North San Juan Fire Hall in his own watershed community (169).

A recent convergence of Snyder's interest in community building, anthropology, and scientific concept and language appears in *Axe Handles*. The volume is dedicated to the place where he lives, San Juan Ridge, in Northern California, which, as noted earlier, he describes in ecological terms as "watershed: west slope of the northern Sierra Nevada, south slope of the east-west running ridge above the south fork, at the level of Back oak mixed with Ponderosa pine."

The first section of the volume, entitled "Loops," has many poems concerned with the "recycling" and "composting" of experience and knowledge. In the title poem, "Axe Handles," Snyder establishes the loop while fashioning a hatchet handle for his son Kai from a broken axe handle, using as the pattern the good handle on the one with which they are chopping wood. Not only is knowledge of handle making passed from father to son, but Snyder is reminded of a fourth-century Chinese essay from which he translates: " 'in making the handle / Of an axe / By cutting wood with an axe / The model is indeed near at hand.' " He remembers, then, too, his own Chinese teacher. And, of course, he knows that he is the model for his own son Kai. The poem concludes by stating that the "energy loop" between past and present, father and son, makes a useful tool for the "craft of culture" which is "[h]ow we go on" (6). In general the poems in the "Loops" section of *Axe Handles* are about the "composting" of his experiences of daily living with family and friends in the watershed community that he knows so well that the "up and down" of the mountains and creeks "stays in my feet" (29). Loops are established between past and present, direct experience and thought, ordinary experience and extraordinary, so that energy pathways are maintained for personal and cultural sustenance.

The last formal part of *Axe Handles* is entitled "Nets," an abbreviation for networks of energy flow. The first cluster of poems is primarily located in nature's networks of energy flow. One, for example, offers glimpses of various creatures in the Yellowstone energy network. Other clusters concentrate on Snyder's involvement with the California Arts Council "network" and on human/nature communities under duress from San Juan Ridge to Alaska and Australia. A final group in the "Nets" section draws together poems that mingle topics and themes familiar to Snyder's readers—from environmental protest in "The Canyon Wren," about rafting down a doomed stretch of the Stanislaus River, to mythic and magical evocations of Indians' ways of understanding nature-life interconnections.

For the scientists Snyder has read, the word "net" has a meaning in addition to network for energy flow. It has the more ordinary meaning of a collecting device like a fishing net.

James Lovelock, author of the Gaia Hypothesis that appeals to the Odums, Margalef, and Snyder—the hypothesis that "the whole of the biosphere is a living organism"—writes that Gaia solved the early evolutionary problem of vital mineral elements being deposited and "trapped" as detritus in sea floor sediments by evolving "chemical and physical nets with which to harvest scarce materials from the sea."[21]

The poet, Snyder argues, is such a net. The poet harvests scarce materials from the detritus of language and myth. A recurrent theme of Snyder's prose and poetry is that the poet salvages and recycles language to capture vital energies that advance us socially and spiritually. Just as "the recycling of dead growth" fosters the health of a natural climax system, poets advance us by "digest[ing] the symbol-detritus" (*RW*, 115–16, 71). Early in his career Snyder had asked himself "just where am I in this food chain" of "poetry, language, myth, symbolism, intellect."[22] Later he learned that the poet digests symbol detritus by "fiddling with the archetypes and getting at people's dreams . . . noting the main structural connections and seeing which parts of the symbol system are no longer useful or applicable. . . . And out of his own vision and hearing of voices he seeks for new paths for the mind-energy to flow" (*RW*, 71). Artistic practice joins spiritual insight since another variant of the "net" is Hua-yen Buddhism's image of Indra's Net, the image evoking the central teaching that "the universe is made not of discrete 'things' as much as knots, or nodes of interrelationship in the endless web of life."[23]

Therefore, the poem itself is a special kind of recycled energy that carries information (or intelligence and wisdom) through the network. Borrowing another idea and phrase from H. T. Odum, Snyder refers to poems as "tiny energies." In a section entitled "Tiny Energies" from the collection *Left Out in the Rain*, Snyder quotes from Odum's *Environment, Power and Society* a passage that had impressed him enough to record it a decade earlier in "The Politics of Ethnopoetics":

> [I]n messages, the energy content as a fuel is far too negligible to measure or consider compared to the great flows of energy in the food chain. Yet the quality of this energy [in messages] (tiny ener-

gies in the right form) is so high that in the right control circuit it may obtain huge amplifications and control vast flows of power.[24]

The energy content of a poem, while slight, can be in a form that makes it so potent that it can overwhelm "vast flows of power" and have enormous cultural and spiritual impact. That is Snyder's hope for poems like the brief "Through" from the "Tiny Energies" section of *Left Out in the Rain*:

> The white spot of a Flicker
> receding through cedar
>
> Fluttering red surveyors tapes
> through trees, the dark woods
> (156)

Energy flow, life, and poetry are inextricably intertwined. The sense of energy surging through everything, human and non-human, material and spiritual, is absolutely central to Gary Snyder's life and work and to his vision of ecological interconnection and interdependence.

While scientific inquiry alone, Snyder has to acknowledge, will not give us "direct knowledge of the forces and energies of the universe," his writings have consistently revealed a fascination with the literal and metaphorical knowledge and insight derived from the ecological sciences (*RW*, 30). Whether thinking about nature, society, or art, he identifies as kindred spirits the ecologists Eugene and Howard T. Odum and Ramon Margalef. In incorporating biological science into his personal mythology, he keeps company with other mid- and late-twentieth-century American writers, such as conservationist Aldo Leopold, nature essayists from Joseph Wood Krutch to Annie Dillard, and poets like himself from A. R. Ammons to Michael McClure. Central to that mythology is a celebration of place that unites the local with the universal, the ordinary with the extraordinary.

It is, of course, not Snyder's intention to celebrate parochialism. A reinhabitation of place that demands an experiential and intellectual knowledge of local biological and geological circumstances and an awareness of the wisdom of peoples who have lived there before is hardly in the service of a provincialism that promotes ignorance of the larger world or hatred of those who live in different ways. On the contrary, Snyder believes, cultural diversity is as important to international stability and health in cultural matters as in the natural world. Moreover, just as it is necessary for us, Snyder says, to absorb the primitive to create a meaningful modern culture but wrong to aspire simply to the primitive, so the reinhabited place is prerequisite to eventual solidarity with people beyond one's own group and to knowing that one's own watershed is part of the larger planetary ecology (*RW*, 172, 173). The poet in touch with the particular energies of place is in touch with the energies of all places. This view is caught in "River in the Valley," which depicts Snyder and his young sons, Gen and Kai, spending a Sunday outdoors exploring California's Sacramento River Valley. When one of his sons asks, "Where do rivers start?" Snyder answers:

> in threads in hills, and gather down to here —
> but the river
> is all of it everywhere,
> all flowing at once,
> all one place.[25]

Expressing the universal-particular paradox, Snyder invites his readers to "find your place on the planet, dig in, and take responsibility from there" (*TI*, 101).

7
Wider Views

The poet says the proper study of mankind is man. I say, study to
forget all that; take wider views of the universe.
—Henry David Thoreau (1854)

There is a common thread that links these scenes and memories—the
spectacle of life in all its varied manifestations as it has appeared,
evolved, and sometimes died out. Underlying the beauty of the
spectacle there is a meaning and significance.
—Rachel Carson (1955)

The informal community of contemporary American writers
whose works of the imagination begin with personal experience in nature deserves recognition. Despite the perennial appeal of their essays, poetry, and fiction to an educated reading
public, these writers are nearly invisible to academics. Literary
historians and historians of popular culture, those academics
most likely to know about "nature writers," tell us little about
them. The writers deserve study individually and as a larger
community. Their "wider views of the universe" are a complex
intellectual and imaginative blend of natural history, human
history, politics, ethics, religion, and biological science. Nineteenth-century romantic ideas, particularly Thoreau's, resur-
face with a new validity and authority conferred by the ecological sciences. So wide are the views that they approach the
mythic, and those who articulate them adopt prophetic
stances. Worried and angry about harm done to the natural
world and its accompanying political and spiritual damage,
these writers, nonetheless, find a measure of hope, a "common
thread" of "meaning and significance."

In Aldo Leopold's and Joseph Wood Krutch's generation
there are, for example, Wallace Stegner, Sigurd Olson, Edwin

Way Teale, Loren Eiseley, and Rachel Carson; a younger generation of well-established writers includes John Haines, Ann Zwinger, Peter Matthiessen, and Edward Hoagland; writers who began publishing after the appearance of a more environmentally aware, post-1960s, audience include Barry Lopez, Richard Nelson, David Rains Wallace, Gretel Ehrlich, Gary Paul Nabhan, and Terry Tempest Williams. As a way to summarize and synthesize my arguments about the kindred spirits who take wider views of the universe than the study of mankind, I will conclude by discussing in some interrelated detail the works of Wallace Stegner, Wendell Berry, and Barry Lopez.

Wallace Stegner's many books, whether novels, histories, biographies, or collections of essays, have as their locus the physical and cultural landscape of the arid West. They include *The Big Rock Candy Mountain* (1943), an autobiographical novel, which sets forth the themes that pervade his life's work, and *Angle of Repose* (1971), for which Stegner received a Pulitzer Prize for fiction; *Beyond the Hundredth Meridian: John Wesley Powell and the Second Opening of the West* (1954), a widely admired work of biography and history; and collections that intermingle history with personal reminiscence, such as *Wolf Willow: A History, a Story, and a Memory of the Last Plains Frontier* (1962), *The Sound of Mountain Water* (1969), and most recently, *Where the Bluebird Sings to the Lemonade Springs: Living and Writing in the West* (1992). His life experiences, from young boyhood in a frontier Saskatchewan prairie town and adolescence in Mormon-settled Salt Lake City, Utah, to later years in California's sophisticated Bay area, intertwined the physical and cultural qualities of this entire century's western American life. He understood his life as an expression of his region:

> If there is such a thing as being conditioned by climate and geography, and I think there is, it is the West that has conditioned me. It has the forms and lights and colors that I respond to in nature and in art. If there is western speech, I speak it; if there is western character or personality, I am some variant of it; if there is a western culture in the small-c, anthropological sense, I have not escaped it. It has to have shaped me. I may even have contributed to it.[1]

He contributed to it. During his repeated explorations of western history, Wallace Stegner sensed that his region has a "geography of hope," that the western stench of vulgarity and rapacity has not obliterated the scent of "prairie flowers and sage brush in which we began," suggesting a "world still nascent, and therefore hopeful."[2] Reaffirming this long-held faith in the West's "geography of hope" in the group of personal essays that begins his most recent book, *Where the Bluebird Sings*, Stegner writes that the essays conclude "with a personal expression of faith in the importance of geography, and especially wilderness, to human personality and culture, that wilderness is the geography of hope for a truly civilized democracy" (11). Critics most often place Stegner in the company of Willa Cather and John Steinbeck, as a regionalist with a national reputation, and with Walter Van Tilburg Clark and A. B. Guthrie, as one who writes historical novels that refuse to accept the sentimental, historically distorted, conventions of the cowboys and Indians "western." But Stegner's understandings of nature's place in human experience and his antimodernist mythmaking bring him also into the company of Leopold, Krutch, Abbey, Dillard, and Snyder.

Stegner's connections with Edward Abbey and Wendell Berry are direct: he was their creative writing mentor in the Stanford University program he led for twenty-five years. Stegner and Berry have written admiringly of each other's work, and Abbey included Stegner in his short list of then-living writers who contribute to "civilization" and cited Stegner's biography of John Wesley Powell, *Beyond the Hundredth Meridian* (1954), as among the most important postwar American books about the West.[3] His connection with these writers, and other kindred spirits, is also manifested by Stegner's recognition of the centrality of Aldo Leopold's "land ethic" in realigning American relationships to nature. "When [our] forming civilization assembles its Bible, its record of the physical and spiritual pilgrimage of the American people, the account of its stewardship in the Land of Canaan," Stegner writes, "*A Sand County Almanac* will belong in it, one of the prophetic books, the utterance of an American Isaiah" (*CSCA*, 233). Acknowledging that Leopold's land ethic is not yet institutionalized, he says it "is not a fact but a task" (245).

Stegner accepted the task of environmental advocacy in the fifties, at the same time as did Joseph Wood Krutch. His baptism was during the 1950s' Dinosaur National Monument battle, which environmental historians regard as a contemporary equivalent to the Hetch Hetchy Dam battle led by John Muir at the turn of the century. Muir's efforts failed to stop construction of the dam that flooded the Tuolumne Valley, equal in beauty to its sister valley in Yosemite National Park. But Stegner, along with other leaders, including the Sierra Club's influential and tireless David Brower, blocked the Upper Colorado River project, which would have dammed the river and flooded Dinosaur National Monument. Encouraged by Brower and supported by the Sierra Club, Stegner edited and contributed chapters to *This Is Dinosaur: Echo Park Country and Its Magic Rivers* (1955), about the beauty and importance of preserving the Dinosaur National Monument wilderness area.[4] The book, distributed to all congressmen and senators, is widely credited by environmental historians with galvanizing the contemporary grass-roots, national, preservationist-conservationist lobby that became the moving force behind the "ecology movement" of the 1960s and 1970s. For more than thirty-five years, until he died in 1993, Stegner took as his citizen's responsibility, both nationally and locally, the role of environmental advocacy and education despite his preference for doing other work. In addition to ceaseless activities on behalf of such organizations as the Audubon Society and the Sierra Club, he published a large number of essays in defense of the land, from his 1960 essay defending "the wilderness *idea* . . . [as] an intangible and spiritual resource"—before such defenses were commonplace—to his "Capsule History of Conservation," which appeared both in *Smithsonian* magazine (1990) and in his most recent collection of essays.[5]

Wallace Stegner's special contribution to this community of writers who love nature was his preoccupation with regional history. He understood it as a story of human successes and failures in using intelligence and imagination to incorporate the special western forms of nature into expressions of a civilization that cherishes them. Acknowledging past and ongoing failures, he kept faith with his belief in the West as having a "geography of hope" that holds a promise for those who exercise moral imagination and communal responsibility.

Beyond the Hundredth Meridian: John Wesley Powell and the Second Opening of the West opens to us Wallace Stegner's larger vision of the proper relationship between humans and nature, a vision that he was articulating in fiction before he wrote the Powell book and continued to develop in the many works that followed. Based on Major Powell's daring 1869 expedition down the Colorado River, through the Grand Canyon, but emphasizing Powell's scientific and experiential knowledge of the West as arid territory, the book portrays Powell as the ideal public servant who was "a champion and instrument of social understanding and social change" (vii). Informed by science and committed to a democratic society, Powell understood that democracy's chances in the West depended on developing social and political institutions suited to life in arid regions, where water rather than land is the essential natural resource. Simply introducing land-wealth–based eastern institutions would invite oligarchic political power held by those who controlled the water supply. Powell's personal ambition was "to see truth and science triumph and the greatest good come to the greatest number over the greatest period of time, according to the American gospels" (viii). Stegner's foil for Powell is William Gilpin, who represents all those who ballyhooed a fantasy-land West that had no relation to the natural conditions determining life in that region. "Romanticizing of the West," Stegner writes, "led to acute political and economic and agricultural blunders, to the sour failure of projects and lives, to the vast and avoidable waste of some resources and the monopolization of others, and to a long delay in the reconciling of institutions to realities" (176).

For Stegner, this tension between Powell and Gilpin symbolizes a persistent tension shaping the history of the West. In Stegner's own life, it was a tension dramatized in his autobiographical novel, *The Big Rock Candy Mountain* (1943). In it the often brutal father uprooted the family to chase the main chance from North Dakota, to Saskatchewan, Washington,

Montana, Utah, Nevada, and California, while the mother longed for "all the beauties and strengths and human associations of place" that Stegner associated with the Mormon community in Salt Lake City.[6] The contemporary descendants of Bo Mason, the character based on Stegner's father, Stegner says, cynically call upon discredited myths to corrupt western politics. Describing themselves as heroes in "sage brush rebellions," these descendants of turn-of-the century "raiders" still maneuver for the "transfer of grazing, timber, oil, or mineral lands from national ownership for the quick profit of a few." They represent, Stegner concludes, "the survival of a gospel that left to its own devices would already have reduced the West to a desert as barren as Syria."[7] While the issue is in doubt between who will finally determine the quality of life in the West, the raiders or democratic citizens committed to the common good, Stegner maintains an optimism he nurtured throughout his fiction, biographies, and histories that the western geography of hope is of two overlapping landscapes: the physical geography of the arid West and the "geography" of the western spirit. In doing so, he created, as have Aldo Leopold, Gary Snyder, and others, a dynamic, life-affirming, myth.

Stegner's work, unlike Annie Dillard's, is not illuminated by mystical responses to nature (even if particular flowers, birds, animals, and weathers are consistently and persistently described in his fiction). He does not call, either, for revolutionary action to overthrow the plunderers as Edward Abbey does (even while continuously unmasking them). Nevertheless, Wallace Stegner is a "seer" who draws upon the combined powers of intelligence, imagination, and art to articulate a hopeful vision that the West will lead us all to a better civilization. In taking a visionary stance, he joins, among others, Aldo Leopold, Joseph Wood Krutch, Annie Dillard, and Gary Snyder. Breaking down distinctions between the personal and the historical, imagined possibility and necessary action, Stegner is a seer with faith that imagination can help bring about a new civilization.[8]

The clearest example of his mythmaking is *Wolf Willow*. Its unfortunate subtitle, "A History, a Story, and a Memoir of the

Last Frontier," was added by an editor. Stegner evokes his geography of hope by nearly erasing such distinctions of genre. The book's three sections, in fact, do not conform to the conventions of genre:

> The first is memory as well as history, and the history is comprehended in terms of what is remembered upon Stegner's return to Saskatchewan. The second part is "a memory" as well as a novella and a short story. The third part is memory, some history, and contemplation—a coming to terms.[9]

This mixture of history, autobiography, and fiction elaborates Stegner's philosophical and experiential point about human connections with a place. *Wolf Willow*, Jamie Robertson concludes, is "Stegner's means of transcending the limitations of civilization for it unifies the human and natural landscape. . . . [The book] is a reenactment of his human connectedness to the earth.[10] Richard W. Etullain, in one of the most perceptive essays about Stegner's vision as historian-novelist, focuses on *Angle of Repose* as a major achievement of mythmaking that takes on the "huge task" of dealing with a century of western history by working brilliantly to elaborate two major thematic dilemmas: "(1) What is the relationship between East and West? . . . and (2) What comparisons and contrasts can be made between the frontier West and the New West of the 1960s?" Stegner demonstrates that "East *and* West . . . the frontier *and* Berkeley generation" make the American West.[11] Most recently Stegner affirmed his faith that humans and nature can be part of a superior civilization, and that the West will produce people with imaginations to show the way, in *Where the Bluebird Sings*:

> I believe that eventually, perhaps within a generation or two, [westerners] will work out some sort of compromise between what must be done to earn a living and what must be done to restore health to the earth, air, and water. I think they will learn to control corporate power and to dampen the excess that has always marked their region, and will arrive at a degree of stability and a reasonably sustainable economy based upon resources that they will know how to cherish and renew. And looking at the western writers, not only [of older generations] but all the new

ones, the Ivan Doigs and Bill Kittredges and James Welches, the
Greta Ehrlichs and Rudolfo Anayas and John Daniels, the Scott
Momadays and Louise Erdrichs and many more, I feel the surge
of the inextinguishable western hope. (xxii)

Although he is not a Westerner, Kentuckian Wendell Berry,
essayist, poet, and novelist, receives some of Wallace Stegner's
highest praise. Stegner opens his essay "The Sense of Place"
with Berry's sentiment that "if you don't know where you are,
. . . you don't know *who* you are," including Berry among
other "lovers of known earth, known weathers, and known
neighbors both human and nonhuman" such as "Thoreau,
Burroughs, Frost, Faulkner, Steinbeck" (199). Wendell Berry,
himself, includes among his literary models Gilbert White, whom
Thoreau admired, as well as Annie Dillard's beloved Henri Fabre.[12] Gary Snyder is among Berry's closest literary friends, to
whom he dedicated *Standing by Words*, which includes the essays
"People, Land, and Community" and "Poetry and Place."

Like the others, Berry is a "placed" person (41). Perhaps
Berry is best known for having "re-inhabited" his family farm,
Lanes Landing, on the Kentucky River. From there he has cel-
ebrated place in widely read volumes of essays such as *The
Long-Legged House* (1969), *A Continuous Harmony* (1972), *The Unsettling of America* (1977), *The Gift of Good Land* (1981), and *Home
Economics* (1988); in fiction, ranging from novels such as *A Place
on Earth* (1967) and *The Memory of Old Jack* (1974) to the "Port
Williams" stories in *The Wild Birds* (1986) and *Fidelity* (1992); and
in nearly two dozen volumes of poems, including *Collected Poems 1957–1982* (1985), *Some Differences* (1987), and *Sabbaths*
(1987). Berry thanks his mentor, Wallace Stegner, for introducing him to "the Great Community" of "recorded human experience" in writing that is not synonymous with "the Pantheon
of Great Writers."[13] That community to which Berry aspired to
contribute, and to which Stegner's writing belongs, includes regional writers who explore the nexus of a particular geography,
its natural history and human history, as well as their own personal experience, both remembered and immediate.

In Berry's "History," a poem dedicated to Wallace Stegner,
the farmer-narrator recounts his re-inhabitation of the land by

farming it, "learning the landmarks and the ways of that land," achieving spiritual contact with the bondsmen settlers and their descendants who for two hundred years "worked and wasted" the farm's slopes. By incorporating the land and its history into his life, the farmer is making "the beginning / of a farm intended to become / my art of being here":

> All the lives this place
> has had, I have. I eat
> my history day by day. . . .
> Now let me feed my song,
> upon the life that is here
> that is the life that is gone.
> This blood has turned to dust
> and liquefied again in stem
> and vein ten thousand times.
> Let what is in the flesh,
> O Muse, be brought to mind.
> (*CP*, 174–75)

For Berry, knowing a piece of land's history, farming its soil respectfully so that it is a legacy worth transmitting, and feeding one's self and family with its products are the conditions for "songs" that join humans with nature and unite past, present, and future. The earth, both domesticated and wild, expressed in one of Berry's favorite tropes, sings through him.

Wendell Berry's stance and voice are prophetic, similar to those of Wallace Stegner, Aldo Leopold, and Gary Snyder. In the "Vision" section of his poem "Work Song," he prophesizes that "a long time after we are dead" our descendants will have rich fields and gardens, a clear river, and an old forest replacing the one "greed and ignorance cut down." The forgotten past will be restored and "memory will grow / into legend, legend into song, song / into sacrament"; "families will be singing in the fields." The "ruined place" will be renewed and enriched. The poet tells us that "This is no paradisal dream. Its hardship is its possibility" (*CP*, 188).

He celebrates the kind of connection with the land Gary Snyder celebrates, melding wild and domestic nature with work, family, friendship, and community.[14] The proximity of

their world views is captured in poems written to each other:
Berry's "To Gary Snyder," recalling the time the two families
were together when wild geese flew over, and Snyder's "Berry
Territory," recalling the discovery of a fox den while walking
with Tanya and Wendell Berry on their farm.[15] The two-word
last line of Snyder's poem resonates with multiple meanings —
"Some home" (the fox den, wild nature, the farm, the commu-
nity of friends). Not surprisingly, Wendell Berry dedicated
Standing by Words to Snyder since its essays include "People,
Land, and Community" and the ambitious "Poetry and Place."
Both writers share an ecological understanding in the largest
sense: natural events have social and spiritual consequences.

While Snyder draws upon scientific language to express an
ecological vision, Berry expresses his own ecological vision
through the metaphor of marriage. Jack Hicks, in his excellent
"Wendell Berry's Husband to the World: *A Place on Earth*" in the
Wendell Berry essay collection, relates the centrality of the marriage metaphor to Berry's literary, moral, and historical vision
(118–34). Hicks writes that

> The model of Berry's own life, recounted in the departures and
> returns to his family and calling and place in *The Long-Legged
> House* and in the recent poetry — especially in his restoration of
> the family Lanes Landing Farm in 1965 — has nourished and been
> nourished by an extraordinary rich metaphor: man as husband,
> in the oldest sense of the word, having committed himself in
> multiple marriages to wife, family, farm, community, and finally
> to the cycle of great nature itself. (119)

Berry's outlook is sacramental, despite an indifference to organized religion characteristic of writers whose visions are
shaped by a profound feeling of connection between humans
and the rest of nature. His relation to the land is holy, and his
vocation, whether expressed in farming or in writing, is to re-
connect holiness with the world, to honor the sabbath by entering "the brotherhood of eye and leaf" in the woods beyond
the "six days' field" through "the narrow gate" where "the
pasture grass of the body's life gives way/ to the high, original
standing of the trees."[16] In the woods he finds grace and the

peace which passeth all understanding, experiences recounted frequently in such poems as "The Peace of Wild Things," which echoes the Twenty-third Psalm:

> When despair for the world grows in me . . .
> I go and lie down where the wood drake
> rests in his beauty on the water, and the great heron feeds.
> I come into the peace of wild things . . .
> I come into the presence of still water . . .
> I rest in the grace of the world, and am free.
>
> (*CP*, 69)

The "husband" participates in the larger mystery of holiness through his relationship with the "close mystery" of nature (121). For the sane, "the world is a holy vision"; and the "ancient faith" is that "what you need is here" (154, 156).

Angry about the strip mining and soil erosion that scar Kentucky hillsides, Wendell Berry is also angry about environmental damage everywhere. He joins Gary Snyder and Edward Abbey, among others, to censure government and large corporations for their indifference and rapacious greed. And he worries about damage ordinary citizens do out of ignorance and laziness. Throughout his poetry, fiction, and essays, Berry persists in asking Aldo Leopold's questions about proper human conduct in nature. In "Getting Along with Nature," he writes that "we do not know how ambitious to be, what or how much we may safely desire, when or where to stop" and have only "nature herself and our cultural traditions" to teach us.[17]

For Berry, as for Annie Dillard, the Christian legacy in American cultural traditions is compatible with establishing a proper relation between humans and nature. Recognizing, however, the failure of Christendom to overcome greed, ignorance, hubris, and sloth, Berry argues in *The Gift of Good Land* (and elsewhere) that biblical tradition calls for a disciplined life which includes practicing an environmental ethic. Christianity can be part of a solution to the environmental crisis. Emphasizing the story of God giving the Promised Land to the Israelites, "a divine gift to a *fallen* people," Berry reasons that we can find the way to ecological discipline in the Bible's development of the relationship between the Israelites and the gift of good land (269). God's grace is revealed in the abilities of a fallen people to exercise stewardship over a gift that can be taken away if they are proven unworthy. Good husbandry ("you may eat the harvest, but you must save seed, and you must preserve the fertility of the fields"); gratitude and humility ("when you have eaten and are satisfied, praise the Lord your God for the good land he has given you"); and good works (nurturing the land for future generations) are the central biblical themes for maintaining harmony among the land, humans, and God (272–73).

Two of Wendell Berry's "Mad Farmer" poems serve to summarize his connections with other writers whose lives and writings are prophetic witness to faith in the possibility of such a harmony. Berry's Mad Farmer persona, a Piers Plowman incarnate, high on holy communion wine, unsettles America by plowing "the churchyard, the minister's wife, three graveyards and a golf course"; the land is replanted with sacred groves of pines and resettled with offspring of the Mad Farmer and the minister's wife, "farmers and their brides sowing and reaping" (CP, 119–20). The poem's title is instructive: "The Mad Farmer Revolution, Being a Fragment of the Natural History of New Eden." Berry's vision is a rebellious, comic, dionysian vision worthy of Edward Abbey and Annie Dillard. In the second poem, "Manifesto: The Mad Farmer Liberation Front," which Berry read in Utah at Edward Abbey's outdoor memorial service, the Mad Farmer exhorts citizens who "love the quick profit, the annual raise, vacation with pay," to "love the Lord" and "love the world," "plant sequoias" and

> Say that your main crop is the forest
> that you did not plant,
> and that you will not live to harvest.
> Say that the leaves are harvested
> when they have rotted into the mold.
> Call that profit. Prophesy such returns.
> Put your faith in the two inches of humus
> that will build under the trees
> every thousand years.

Above all, "Practice resurrection" (CP, 151–52). The voice is undeniably Berry's but also Abbey's, Snyder's, Dillard's, Krutch's, and Leopold's.

Barry Lopez, one of Wendell Berry's admirers and another kindred spirit, practices resurrection. At the conclusion of *Arctic Dreams: Imagination and Desire in a Northern Landscape* (1986), which won the National Book Award, he records his glimpse of redeemed humans in harmony with nature as he looks out over the Bering Sea and bows with respect and reverence "to what knows no deliberating legislature or parliament, no religion, no competing theories of economics, an expression of allegiance with the mystery of life" (414). The physical landscape and his dream of finding "a dignity that might include all living things," are fused through an act of imagination (404). One of the highest expressions of human evolution, Lopez writes, is "the continuous work of the imagination . . . to bring what is actual together with what is dreamed" (414). Standing at the edge of the water, gulls overhead, gray whales present but out of sight, remembering details of the morning walk, he experiences his mind emptying as "the edges of the real landscape became one with the edges of something I had dreamed," and he achieves a momentary state in which "light is unbounded, nurturing, suffused with wisdom and creation, a state in which one has absorbed that very darkness which before was the perpetual sign of defeat" (414). An earlier passage in *Arctic Dreams* provides a gloss for his experience when he refers to the eleventh and twelfth centuries as "an age of visionaries who spoke of the New Jerusalem of the Apocalypse, where there would be no darkness," a time when God and the "*relationship* between God and man was light" (248). He believes that as a species we should trust our future to an intelligence that is not reason alone but a "desire to embrace and be embraced in the pattern that both theologians and physicists call God," hoping that "intelligence, in other words, is love" (250).

Lopez's natural history essays, folklore, and fiction have consistently probed ways the imagination can find redemptive wisdom while drawing attention to signs of moral and political failure. In addition to *Arctic Dreams*, they include *Desert Notes: Reflections in the Eye of a Raven* (1976), *Giving Birth to Thunder, Sleeping with His Daughter: Coyote Builds North America* (1978), *Of*

Wolves and Men (1978), *River Notes: The Dance of Herons* (1979), *Winter Count* (1981), *Crossing Open Ground* (1988), *Crow and Weasel* (1990), and *The Rediscovery of North America* (1990). The movement from alienation to affirmative wisdom occurs through an integration or distillation of a range of information and ideas accruing most notably from Western science, anthropology, and personal experience, the categories familiar to readers of contemporary literature based in nature—variants of Gary Snyder's recommendation to learn the flowers and know the lore. The sources for *Arctic Dreams*, for example, are not only Lopez's wide reading but his travels with marine ecologists, Eskimos hunters, Canadian landscape painters, oil crew roughnecks, and others who project their dreams upon the arctic landscape. In four or five years of traveling in the Arctic, he came to believe that "people's desires and dreams were as much a part of the land as the wind, solitary animals, and the bright fields of stone and tundra" and that "we have been telling ourselves the story of what *we* represent in the land for 40,000 years" at the heart of which is "a simple, abiding belief: it is possible to live wisely on the land, and to live well" (xxii, xxviii).

Lopez dramatically presents the need for redemptive wisdom. "The Passing Wisdom of Birds" in *Crossing Open Ground* recounts Hernando Cortes's terrorist act on June 16, 1520, of setting fire to Mexico City's splendid aviaries housing thousands of egrets, wrens, thrushes, parrots, humming birds, and condors. It is a central horrific example for Lopez of "a kind of destructive madness that lies at the heart of imperialistic conquest" and "a symbol of a long-term failure of Western civilization to recognize the intrinsic worth of the American landscape" (196, 197). In his most recent volume, *The Rediscovery of North America*, Lopez deftly and powerfully associates the greed behind Spanish atrocities against land and people in the New World with the greed motivating nineteenth-century American pioneers on the Oregon Trail. Their greed, he continues in a personal note, reverberates today in "the rhetoric of timber barons in my home state of Oregon, standing before the last of the old-growth forest, irritated that anyone is saying *'enough'* " (10).

Not lost in anger and despair, Barry Lopez as a writer becomes the healing shaman and prophet, a stance similar to, among others, Leopold's, Abbey's, Dillard's, and Snyder's. Lopez takes on the shaman's work of repairing "a spirit in disarray."[18] Lopez's books, Sherman Paul argues, engage us in "the exegesis of the soul" and his landscapes are "places of vision quest and shamanic flight."[19] Lopez, himself, in "Landscape and Narrative," distinguishes between two landscapes—the outer and the inner, the outer one of weather, plants, animals, and geology and the inner landscape that is "a kind of projection within a person of a part of the exterior landscape" that depends on "one's moral, intellectual, and spiritual development." As healing shaman, storyteller, Lopez's objective is to bring the two landscapes together for himself and others, thereby repairing the spirit by "reproducing the harmony of the land in the individual's interior."[20]

While the metaphors Aldo Leopold uses for encouraging new human-nature relations are drawn from democratic and religious traditions, Gary Snyder's from the ecological sciences, and Wendell Berry's from husbandry, Barry Lopez's are drawn from the language of intimate friendship. In *Arctic Dreams*, landscapes like the Arctic, which "initially appear barren . . . can open suddenly, like the corolla of a flower, when any intimacy with it is sought" (xiv). So he cultivates that intimacy through "conversation with the land," a phrase be borrowed from Canadian geologist and landscape painter Maurice Haycock (226). We need to "approach the land as we would a person, by opening an intelligent conversation" based upon the assumption that the other conversationalist is more complex and interesting than we could imagine.[21] We need to listen: asking a man in Anaktuvuk Pass what he does when he enters a new place, Lopez was told, "I listen" (275). Looking upon the land as a companion, cultivating its intimacy, and engaging it in conversation will, over years and through generations, tell the story of how to "live wisely on the land, and to live well."

Lopez's literary activity is, of course, a spiritual and moral activity. By his efforts to bring the outer and inner landscape together through acts of the imagination Lopez is conjoining ecological science and romantic insight. Speaking of a wisdom to be found in the landscape, Lopez says that "we have a science of ecology that allows us to put all the named things in some kind of grand order" but "a lot that goes on out there is invisible to us . . . . Some of it's visible to science, some of it's visible to mystics, some of it's visible to local inhabitants but much of it is unreachable, uncontainable." The order in nature—revealed partially through ecological science, partially through everyday living in nature, and partially through mystical experience—is "a part of what we call 'God.' It is the face of God."[22]

How are we to come to know the land and grow spiritually so that we heal it and ourselves, he asks in *The Rediscovery of North America* (31). His answers resonate with Leopold's, Berry's, Snyder's, and those of other kindred spirits. For example, Lopez's exhortation to "look upon the land not as its possessor but as a companion" echoes Leopold's injunction to cease being a conqueror and become a citizen; his encouragement to take up "residence in a place" such as "the basin of the Kentucky River" and learn the local history alludes transparently to Wendell Berry's example; and his recommendations to "read in the anthropological and archeological literature about those we moved out of our way," to memorize and remember the land by walking it, eating "from its soils and from the animals that ate its plants" and observing the sequence of its flowers and range of birds, are identical to Snyder's recommendations (32–34). Lopez's outlook is strikingly similar to theirs, and throughout *Rediscovery of North America* he refers to others who are kindred spirits: Loren Eiseley, Thomas Merton, Richard Nelson, and Gary Nabhan, for example. Tellingly, the book is dedicated to Rachel Carson. Sounding like Wallace Stegner and Edward Abbey, Lopez states that these writers produce a "literature of hope" that is an "antidote to solipsism." He even recognizes these writers as a group with goals that transcend individual literary ambitions, pointing out that his colleagues and friends among nature writers "have a genuine affection for each other" and support and respect one another's work.[23]

Like other writers in this study, Barry Lopez urgently seeks to tell this story. Failure to converse with the land and to tell its story has devastating intellectual, social, and political consequences: "reductionism in science; fundamentalism in religion; fascism in politics." Success, though, may be possible. To achieve it Lopez recommends a "modern realignment with the natural world" based upon work by field biologists, natural geographers, anthropologists living among hunter-gatherer peoples, and philosophers such as "Aldo Leopold and Rachel Carson," who include the "indispensable element of personal experience."[24]

He could just as well have added other writers whose imaginations, like his own, grasp a common narrative in the seemingly separate endeavors of those biologists, anthropologists, and philosophers. Barry Lopez takes his place among the best writers who are preoccupied with nature and who are attempting to articulate integrating visions. In his Eskimo legends, Narwhal migrations, iceberg mountains, and extraordinary light of *Arctic Dreams*, radically different regions border one another. "In biology these transitional areas between two different communities are called ecotones," Lopez notes, and he is drawn to those exciting edges (123). The edges he "walks" are more than ecological, however; they are thin boundaries between human and nonhuman, between knowledge and mystery, between the mundane and the sacred. That which can be known from scientific study is essential knowledge—*Arctic Dreams* is studded with scientific allusions in text, appendices, and bibliography; direct experience is likewise crucial—like Snyder, Lopez learns by walking, eating, working. No matter how accurate the scientific study of any piece of land or how completely lived in it is, knowledge of that land, Lopez claims, will be inadequate. We have, therefore, an obligation to approach the land with an "uncalculating mind, with an attitude of regard," that leaves room for mystery. As have the others in this community of kindred spirits, Lopez humbly prepares for "that moment when something sacred reveals itself within the mundane" (228).

At that moment, in any intimately known landscape, Barry Lopez is as much at "home" as Wallace Stegner in the Great Basin or, more obviously, Wendell Berry at Lanes Landing Farm, Kentucky, or Gary Snyder at Kitkitdizze in the Shasta Nation of Turtle Island. Even the earliest figures among nature

writers, from Cadwallader Colden and John Bartram to Thomas
Nuttall and John James Audubon, Lopez comments, are misunderstood as providing a "kind of entertainment" when, in
fact, they were providing "a description of home."[25] As Robert
Finch says succinctly, "[N]ature writers teach us to recognize
home."[26] That is, of course, true of the writers central to this
study. Aldo Leopold lived upon and wrote about eighty acres
of "useless" land in "Sand County" Wisconsin. He respected
and loved that "community" and it produced cultural and aesthetic harvests. A conservationist, he thought in terms of a history that included the story of interactions between humans
and the land and struggled to articulate an ethical framework
for land use as a prerequisite for intelligent public policy. Joseph Wood Krutch, Leopold's popularizer, experienced a sense
of homecoming in the desert around Tucson, Arizona. His
study of the animals, birds, insects, and plants with whom he
shared life there led him to conclude that humanistic values
such as love, courage, and intelligence, which were losing their
potency in modern belief systems, were not only vital but visible in nonhuman lives as well, a cause for joyous celebration.
Fellow southwesterner Edward Abbey felt most at home in
landscapes as austere and indifferent to human survival as
those portrayed earlier by Jack London and Robinson Jeffers.
Taking responsibility for his home means acting on the anarchist faith that the powers of State, industry, and the military
are vulnerable to the collective wit and actions of those who
love the land. Annie Dillard, at creekside in Virginia, found a
backyard cedar transfigured into a flaming revelation; and on
the shores of Puget Sound, she experienced the Sound as a god
who awakened her with a kiss, embraced the Pacific Ocean,
and, finally, held all of nature. Her responsibility is to pray,
saying "glory" and "amen." Snyder, a citizen of Turtle Island,
digs in by using ecology literally, metaphorically, and mythically to bring into congruence the prehistoric and historic, matter and spirit, nature and society, the self and the other.

This community of contemporary American writers whose
personae unite the personal with the prophetic and ordinary
experience with the millennial, sustains a vision that counters
mainstream alienation, fragmented sensibility, self-interested

politics, and spiritual confusion. Its members realize that unless we understand the natural condition ecologically, the human condition is unfathomable. Their integrating visions bring
into harmony inner and outer landscapes, the natural, social,
and spiritual realms. Most simply, they have all learned what
kindred spirit Terry Tempest Williams divined when some Na-
vajo children asked her "what story does [the yucca plant]
tell?" "Everything is subject to story," she realized; "everything is related." If you are receptive and open, "you realize
you are in the service or attendance of something . . . much
larger than yourself."[27]

NOTES

BIBLIOGRAPHY

INDEX

Notes

Chapter 1. Kindred Spirits

1. Aldo Leopold, "Foreword" (1947), reprinted in *CSCA*, 287.
2. John D. Margolis, *Joseph Wood Krutch: A Writer's Life* (Knoxville: University of Tennessee Press, 1980), 151; quoted in Margolis, 151.
3. Joseph Wood Krutch, *Henry David Thoreau* (New York: William Sloane, 1948), 184.
4. Ibid., 67.
5. *The New West of Edward Abbey* (Albuquerque: University of New Mexico Press, 1982), 129.
6. Abbey elsewhere refers to this endnote and this line from Thoreau (*DR*, 36).
7. *PTC*, 148; *Walden*, J. Lyndon Shanley, ed. (Princeton: Princeton University Press, 1973), 318.
8. Mary Davidson McConahay, " 'Into the Bladelike Arms of God': The Quest for Meaning through Symbolic Language in Thoreau and Annie Dillard," *Denver Quarterly* 20 (1985): 107.
9. "Natural History of Massachusetts," *Henry David Thoreau: The Natural History Essays*, Robert Sattelmeyer, ed. (Salt Lake City: Peregrine Smith, 1980), 28.
10. *"Pilgrim at Tinker Creek* and the Burden of Science," *American Literature* 59 (1) (Mar. 1987): 84.
11. Bob Steuding, *Gary Snyder* (Boston: Twayne, 1976), 115, 118.
12. The best account of this history is in *NE*; see also *RN*, 55–59.
13. Donald Worster argues that a distinguishing feature of this strain of contemporary ecological thinking is more mechanistic than organic: for ecologists from Tansley, who want to quantify ecological relationships, to postwar ecologists such as, most notably, Eugene Odum, a bioeconomics paradigm rules. But, as the work of Howard T. Odum shows, the patterns of energy flowing through nature suggest for some scientists and, as Worster states, for many nonscientists, an organic model of nature. See, for example, Odum's *Environ-*

ment, *Power and Society* (New York: Wiley-Interscience, 1971). This topic is discussed more fully in Chapter 6.

14. McIlroy, *"PTC and Burden,"* 77–78.

15. "The Joys of Reading," *New York Times Magazine* (16 May 1982), 47; Ann Haven Morgan, *Field Book of Ponds and Streams: An Introduction to the Life of Fresh Water* (New York: Putnam's, 1930).

16. McIlroy, *"PTC and Burden,"* 82.

17. *The Modern Temper* (New York: Harcourt, Brace & World, 1956), xi.

Chapter 2. Aldo Leopold: Mythmaker

1. Gifford Pinchot, *The Fight for Conservation* (New York: Doubleday, Page, 1910), quoted in Donald Worster, *American Environmentalism: The Formative Period, 1860-1915* (New York: Wiley, 1973), 85.

2. Susan L. Flader, *Thinking Like a Mountain* (Columbia: University of Missouri Press, 1974), 24.

3. In the language and concepts, one can see the importance of Frederic Clements's organismic ideas about climax communities and his critic Arthur Tansley's ideas about energy flow as well as Elton's concepts. For a more complete discussion of their importance to Leopold, see Flader, *Thinking Like a Mountain* and "Introduction," *RMG,* 4–8. See Chapter 6 below for a discussion of similar ideas and metaphors in Gary Snyder's essays and poetry.

4. For a fuller accounting of references to Leopold as prophet see *RMG,* 30, n. 20.

5. Aldo Leopold, "Charles Knesal Cooperrider, 1889–1944," *Journal of Wildlife Management,* 12 (3) (July 1948): 337–39.

6. *Nature Writing and America* (Ames: Iowa State University Press, 1990), 193.

7. "The Husbandry of the Wild," *For the Love of the World: Essays on Nature* (Iowa City: University of Iowa Press, 1992), 46.

8. Sherman Paul identifies the Heidegger connection (*For the Love of the World,* 42). See Chapter 6 below for a discussion of "re-inhabitation."

9. Ibid., 60.

10. Lester Ward, *The Psychic Factors of Civilization* (Boston: Ginn & Co., 1893), quoted in Worster, *American Environmentalism,* 49, 47.

11. In *Thinking Like a Mountain,* Susan Flader provides an excellent account of the gradual intellectual development that brought Leopold to a biocentric, ecological outlook. The essay in *SCA,* is, of course, a presentation of its personal, spiritual impact upon him. See John Tall-

madge for another reading of this essay as a "conversion" experience (*CSCA*, 125–27).

12. *Pine Cone* (July 1919), quoted in *AL*, 174.

13. *The Twelve Seasons* (New York: William Sloane), 13.

14. The ecological ideas and images reveal Leopold's continuing indebtedness not only to Elton's ideas about community but to Clements's organicist ideas about the features of "climax" communities which no longer have wide acceptance among ecologists. The "fountain of energy" image would find wider acceptance since contemporary, "new ecologists" measure energy flow through systems and can trace their ecological heritage back to Arthur G. Tansley, with whose work Leopold was familiar. See Leopold's 1939 essay, "A Biotic View of Land," which prefigures "The Land Ethic" and includes this quoted material (reprinted in *RMG*, 266–73). Twenty-five years after the publication of "The Land Ethic," Gary Snyder drew from these early ecological ideas recast by major postwar ecologist Eugene Odum (see Chapter 6).

15. "Some Fundamentals of Conservation in the Southwest," *Environmental Ethics* 1 (Summer 1979): 138; reprinted in *RMG*, 86–97. See also, "The Forestry of the Prophets" (1920), reprinted in *RMG*, 71–77.

16. *Science* 155 (1967): 1203–7.

17. "Some Fundamentals," 140.

18. *Earth Rising: Ecological Belief in an Age of Science* (Corvallis: Oregon State University Press, 1989), 42.

19. "1947 Foreword," *CSCA*, 285; see also "Conservationist in Mexico" (1937), reprinted in *RMG*, 239–44.

20. Oates, *Earth Rising*, 171.

21. *John Muir and His Legacy* (Boston: Little Brown, 1981), 359.

22. Quoted in Joseph M. Petulla, *American Environmentalism: Values, Tactics, Priorities* (College Station: Texas A & M University Press, 1980), 4.

23. *Man's Responsibility for Nature: Ecological Problems and Western Traditions* (New York: Scribner, 1974), 123.

24. *Ethics* 85 (1975): 101.

25. "The Interrelationship of Ecological Science and Environmental Ethics," *Environmental Ethics* 1 (Fall 1979): 199, 201.

26. *Environmental Ethics* 1 (Fall 1979): 221.

27. See Nash, "Liberating Nature," *RN*, 161–98.

Chapter 3. Joseph Wood Krutch: Metabiologist

1. John D. Margolis, *Joseph Wood Krutch*, 187; "Prologue," *GANW*, 73.

2. *The Modern Temper*, 169.

3. *Henry David Thoreau*, 184.

4. "William Morton Wheeler," an appreciation signed by L. J. Henderson, Thomas Barbour, F. M. Carpenter, and Hans Zimmer in *EPB*.

5. Quoted in *GANW*, 73; see also *MLO*, 333 and elsewhere.

6. Mary Alice Evans and Howard Ensign Evans, *William Morton Wheeler, Biologist* (Cambridge: Harvard University Press, 1970), 223.

7. "The Stubborn Fact of Consciousness," *The Measure of Man: On Freedom, Human Values, Survival and the Modern Temper* (Indianapolis: Bobbs Merrill, 1954), 122.

8. *Measure of Man*, 120.

9. *Measure of Man*, 123, 130–32.

10. *The Great Chain of Life* (Boston: Houghton Mifflin, 1956), x.

11. That other scientists, as well as lay persons, remain fascinated by the possibility that animals can think is indicated by Eugene Linden's cover story, "Can Animals Think?", *Time* (Mar. 22, 1993): 54–61.

12. *Animal Thinking* (Cambridge: Harvard University Press, 1984), iv.

13. *The Question of Animal Awareness* (New York: Rockefeller University Press, 1976), 85.

14. *Animal Thinking*, 69.

15. Ibid., 70.

16. "Wilderness as More Than Tonic," *If You Don't Mind My Saying So* (New York: William Sloane, 1965), 368, 390 *passim; Great Chain of Life*, 120. See, for example, Sinnott, *The Biology of the Spirit* (New York: Viking, 1955).

17. His first expression of mystical pantheism is in the awkward but revealing essay for January, "God's Great Owl," *Twelve Seasons*. See especially, 153–54.

18. "Birds and Airplanes," *A Krutch Omnibus: Forty Years of Social and Literary Criticism* (New York: William Morrow, 1970), 339–40.

19. *Evolution: The History of an Idea* (Berkeley, University of California Press, 1984), 309. For a history of analogous tensions among ecologists that continue today, see Daniel Botkin, *Discordant Harmonies* (New York: Oxford University Press, 1991); Robert McIntosh, *The Background of Ecology* (New York: Cambridge University Press, 1985); and *NE*. Understanding these tensions between reductionists and their critics, such as leading postwar "new ecologist" Eugene Odum, is valuable for understanding Gary Snyder's work (See Chapter 6 below).

Chapter 4. *Edward Abbey: An "Earthiest"*

1. "Immigration and Liberal Taboos," *OL*, 41–44; "The Future of Sex: A Reaction to a Pair of Books—Brownmiller's *Feminity* and Steinem's *Outrageous Acts*," *OL*, 199–205.
2. *A Voice Crying in the Wilderness* (New York: St. Martin's Press, 1990), 3, 5, 9.
3. *The New West of Edward Abbey*, 137.
4. Ibid., 139, 145.
5. *Nature Writing and America*, 289.
6. For lists Abbey made of writers he admired, see *AR*, xix–xxi; *JH*, xii; *OL*, 170–78.
7. Joan London, *Jack London and His Times: An Unconventional Biography* (New York: Book League of America, 1939), 209.
8. Richard Shelton, "Creeping Up on *Desert Solitaire*," *RM*, 69.
9. *Beyond the Wall* (New York: Holt Rinehart & Winston, 1984), 194–95.
10. See especially, Earl Labor, *Jack London* (New York: Twayne Publishers, 1974), and James I. McClintock, *White Logic: Jack London's Short Stories* (Grand Rapids: Wolf House Books, 1975).
11. *John Barleycorn* (New York: Century Company, 1913), 112–13.
12. *New West of Edward Abbey*, 86–87.
13. Ibid., 91, 79.
14. *Children of the Frost* (New York: Macmillan, 1902), 37–38.
15. "Come On In," *JH*, 87; *White Logic*, 36 *passim*.
16. "Science with a Human Face," *AR*, 125.
17. "What Life Means to Me," quoted in Philip S. Foner, *Jack London, American Rebel* (New York: Citadel Press, 1947), 396; Sam Baskett, ed., *Martin Eden*, (New York: Rinehart, 1956), 212.
18. Gordon Mills, "The Symbolic Wilderness: James Fenimore Cooper and Jack London," *Nineteenth Century Fiction* 13 (March 1959): 152.
19. *White Logic*, 82; *First Principles of a New System of Philosophy* (New York, 1987), 76.
20. *White Logic*, 83.
21. *Beyond the Wall*, 154.
22. "Edward Abbey, American: Another Radical Conservative," *Denver Quarterly* 12 (4) (1978): 11.
23. For the best discussion of the Abbey-Jeffers relations, see Diane Wakoski, "Edward Abbey: Joining the Visionary 'Inhumanists,'" *RM*, 102–7.

24. *Roan Stallion, Tamar, and Other Poems* (New York: Modern Library, 1935), 295.

25. "How to See It," *The Desert Year* (New York: William Sloane, 1952), 38.

26. *Cawdor and Other Poems* (New York: Horace Liveright, 1928), 154; "Serpents of Paradise," 17.

27. Jeffers, "Life from the Lifeless," *Selected Poetry* (New York: Random House, 1935), 564.

28. *Double Axe* (New York: Random House, 1948), vii.

29. "Carmel Point," quoted in *OL*, 72; originally in Jeffers, *Solstice* (1935).

30. *DS*, 132; *Roan Stallion*, 97.

31. "The Answer," *Selected Poetry*, 594.

32. David Solheim and Rob Levin, "The *Bloomsbury Review* Interview," *RM*, 79–91.

33. Les Stamford, "Desert Places: An Exchange with Edward Abbey," *Western Humanities Review* 24 (Autumn 1970): 396.

34. An earlier version of this novel appeared as the novella *Confessions of a Barbarian* (Santa Barbara: Capra Press, 1986).

35. At rare moments Traven does focus on the land and human abuses of it. In *Treasure of the Sierra Madre*, for example, when Dobbs asks why they must return the mountainside they have been mining to its original state, Howard answers, "The Lord might have said it's only a waste of time to build this earth, if it was He who actually did it. I figure we should be thankful to the mountain which has rewarded our labor so generously. So we shouldn't leave this place as careless picnic parties and dirty motorists so often do. We have wounded this mountain and I think it is our duty to close its wounds. The silent beauty of this place deserves our respect . . . I'm sorry we can't do this restoration perfectly—that we can do no better than show our good intention and our gratitude." (New York: Knopf, 1936), 189–90.

36. Gregory McNamee, "Scarlet 'A' on a Field of Black," *RM*, 25.

37. Quoted in Michael L. Baumann, *B. Traven, An Introduction* (Abuquerque: University of New Mexico Press, 1976), 79.

38. Ibid.

39. See *The Myth of the Machine*, vol. 1, *Technics and Human Development* (New York: Harcourt, Brace and World, 1964), and vol. 2, *The Pentagon of Power* (1970). Abbey includes Mumford in his list of writers who have contributed to "civilization."

40. Peter Wild, *Pioneer Conservationists of Western America* (Missoula, Mont., 1979), xvii, quoted in *RN*, 168.

41. *DS*, 208; *Hayduke Lives!*, 292.

Chapter 5. Annie Dillard: Ritualist

1. Dillard has been a contributing editor for *Harper's Magazine* and has taught creative writing at various colleges and universities. She received a Pulitzer Prize in 1974 for *Pilgrim at Tinker Creek*. Her books on other subjects are: *Tickets for a Prayer Wheel* (Columbia: University of Missouri Press, 1974); *Living by Fiction* (New York: Harper & Row, 1982); *Encounters with Chinese Writers* (Middletown, Conn.: Wesleyan University Press, 1984); *An American Childhood* (New York: Harper & Row, 1987); and *The Writing Life* (New York: Harper & Row, 1989).

2. Abbey's most direct comment on "Mystery . . . with an emphatically capital M" occurs in "The Ancient Dust," *Beyond the Wall*, 154.

3. "The Historical Roots of Our Ecological Crisis," *Science* 155 (1967): 1203–7.

4. *John Muir and His Legacy*, 363, 358.

5. Adams quoted in *John Muir*, 363.

6. Ibid., 365.

7. *A Continuous Harmony* (New York: Harcourt Brace Jovanovich, 1972), 5, 66.

8. *An American Childhood*, 133.

9. Nancy Lucas, "Annie Dillard," *Dictionary of Literary Biography Yearbook: 1980* (Detroit: Gale Research Co., 1981), 187; quoted in William J. Scheick, "Annie Dillard, Narrative Fringe," *Contemporary American Women Writers: Narrative Strategies*, Catherine Rainwater and William J. Scheick, eds. (Lexington: University of Kentucky Press, 1985), 63; Scheick, 61.

10. "The Artist as Nun: Theme, Tone and Vision in the Writings of Annie Dillard," *Studia Mystica* 1 (4) (1978): 18.

11. Margaret Loewen Reimer, "The Dialectical Visions of Annie Dillard's *Pilgrim at Tinker Creek*," *Critique* 24 (1983): 189.

12. *An American Childhood*, 132–33, 227–28.

13. *PTC*, 342; David L. Lavery, "Noticer: The Visionary Art of Annie Dillard," *Massachusetts Review* 21 (1980): 257.

14. Tom Wolf, "A New Walk Is a New Walk," *Walking Magazine* (Autumn 1986), 64–65, 65.

15. *Henry David Thoreau: The Natural History Essays*, 93, 135–36.

16. *Imagining the Earth* (Urbana: University of Illinois Press), 99, 100.

17. "The Bridge to Heaven," *Islands, the Universe, Home* (New

York: Viking, 1991), 97. See Alan Williamson's Zen Buddhist reading of "A Walk" in Jon Halper, ed., *Gary Snyder: Dimensions of a Life* (San Francisco: Sierra Club Books, 1991), 216–30.

18. *Desert Year*, 38.

19. Emerson (1836) quoted in John Conron, ed., *The American Landscape* (New York: Oxford University Press, 1974), 581.

20. See McIlroy, *"Pilgrim at Tinker Creek* and the Burden of Science," and Reimer, "Dialectical Vision."

21. Dillard is unaware that this popular conception is no longer a scientific view.

22. Alexander Teixeira de Mattos, trans., *The Insect World of J. Henri Fabre* (New York: Dodd, Mead, 1961).

23. *Encyclopedia Britannica*, 15th ed., s.v. "Heraclitus."

24. *Holy the Firm*, 45; Scheick, "Annie Dillard," 58.

25. *Holy the Firm*, 77.

Chapter 6. Gary Snyder: Posthumanist

1. "Does Bioregionalism Need an Open Fire (Wildfire) (Control Burn)?" *Raise the Stakes, the Planet Drum Review*, no. 10 (Summer 1984): 3; "What's Meant by 'Here,' " *TI*, 112. A nearly identical address appears in *PW*, 41.

2. James M. Houston, "The Concepts of 'Place' and 'Land' in the Judeo-Christian Tradition," *Humanistic Geography: Prospects and Problems*, David Ley and Marwyn Samuels, eds. (Chicago: Maaroufa Press, 1978), 226.

3. *Regarding Wave* (New York: New Directions, 1967), 40.

4. Anon., *Choice* 9 (March 1972): 82.

5. Another scientist important to Snyder is California conservationist Raymond Dasmann. Two anthologies of essays about energy by physical and social scientists made strong impressions on Snyder's work: John Holdren and Philip Herrera's *energy* and *Energy and Power*, a *Scientific American* anthology (San Francisco: W. H. Freeman 1971).

6. *Fundamentals of Ecology* (New York: Holt, Rinehart & Winston, 1963), 39.

7. *Regarding Wave*, 17.

8. Many contemporary ecologists would not make such a sweeping claim for succession, preferring to state simply that succession is "the process of development (or redevelopment) of an ecosystem over time"; no claim is made for climax states presenting maximum diversity and stability (Daniel B. Botkin, *Discordant Harmonies*, 231).

Botkin and historian of science Robert P. McIntosh (*The Background of Ecology*) provide accounts of such divisions in the development of the ecological sciences which began early in the century and continue today and can be traced to differences between Frederic Clements and Herbert Gleason. While Clements argued from an organic view of nature, which included the idea that collections of plant species occurring together behave as a "superorganism" and grow to a stable and diverse climax condition, Gleason has an individualistic view of nature that "suggested that the climax was a haphazard, imperfect, and shifting organization–one that man need not worry overly much about disturbing" (*NE*, 239). See McIntosh for a particularly succinct and clear account of differences between Clementsians and Gleasonians (76–85).

Significantly, Snyder draws most heavily upon Eugene Odum, who in the 1950s presented a Clementsian emphasis on organismic community and succession to stable climax in one of the most successful textbooks on ecology (McIntosh, 82).

9. These three ecologists were leaders in the postwar development of the "New Ecology" (Botkin noting that Eugene Odum is considered by many the "father of modern ecosystem ecology"), emphasizing "energetics" by quantifying the flow of energy through ecosystems. This major shift from Leopold's biotic model for ecology to an energy-economic model in the postwar period can be interpreted as a triumph of mathematical ecologists and reductionists over holists. Worster takes E. P. Odum as the postwar leader in this change, and notes that his energetics model emphasizes "the flow of goods and services—or of energy—in a kind of automated, robotized, pacified nature" that is "perfectly tailored for the needs of a modern-day Ely or Pinchot" (*NE*, 313, 312). But, as McIntosh points out, E. P. Odum managed to combine his leadership in energetics with a continuing Clementsian holism: "Odum . . . allowed that science should be both reductionist and holist, but made clear that there has been enough of the former and too little of the latter" (*Background of Ecology*, 252). While most New Ecologists reject Clementsian organism and holism, Odum gave them some continuing respectability. For nonscientist Snyder, Odum's views are scientifically acceptable as well as philosophically and politically compatible with his own views in ways that other reductionist, contemporary ecological positions cannot be. Finally, Odum's model does not present a "pacified" nature to Snyder; instead, it presents a nature coursing with energy that is analogous to energy flowing through the body (organicism) and analogous to the spirit of "no nature."

10.   Margalef, *Perspectives in Ecological Theory*, (Chicago: University of Chicago Press, 1968), 29.

11.   *Environment, Power and Society*, 15.

12.   *Axe Handles* (San Francisco: North Point Press, 1983), 105–6.

13.   *Ecology: The Link between the Natural and the Social Sciences*, 2d ed. (New York: Holt, Rinehart & Winston, 1975), 74. The significant subtitle was added with this edition.

14.   *Environment, Power and Society*, vii.

15.   *He Who Hunted Birds in His Father's Village: The Dimensions of a Haida Myth* (Bolinas, Calif.: Grey Fox Press, 1979).

16.   *In Search of the Primitive: A Critique of Civilization* (New Brunswick, N.J.: Transaction Press, 1974), quoted in *Earth House Hold*, 126.

17.   "Good, Wild, Sacred," *CoEvolution Quarterly*, no. 39 (Fall 1983): 17.

18.   No. 6 in "Hunting" section, *Myths & Texts*.

19.   *He Who Hunted Birds*, 93–95.

20.   *Earth House Hold*, 122.

21.   J. E. Lovelock, *Gaia: A New Look at Life on Earth* (New York: Oxford University Press, 1989), 26.

22.   *Earth House Hold*, 3.

23.   David Barnhill, "A Giant Act of Love: Reflections on the First Precept," *Tricycle: The Buddhist Review* 11 (3) (Spring 1993): 29.

24.   *Left Out in the Rain*, 153; *OW*, 40; *Environment, Power and Society*, 171.

25.   *Axe Handles*, 9.

Chapter 7. Wider Views

1.   *Where the Bluebird Sings* (New York: Random House, 1992).

2.   *Sound of Mountain Water* (Garden City, N.Y.: Doubleday, 1969), 171.

3.   Stegner, "A Letter to Wendell Berry," *Where the Bluebird Sings*, 207–13; Wendell Berry, "Wallace Stegner and the Great Community," *What Are People For?* (San Francisco: North Point Press, 1990), 48–57.

4.   For more about Stegner's involvement with this and other conservation issues, see Stegner and Richard W. Etulian, "The Wilderness West," *Conversations with Wallace Stegner* (Salt Lake City: University of Utah Press, 1984), 167–83.

5.   "Coda, Wilderness Letter," *Conversations with Wallace Stegner*, 145–53; *Where the Bluebird Sings*, 117–32.

6.   *Where the Bluebird Sings*, 33; Stegner wrote two histories about

that Mormon community: *Mormon Country* (New York: Duell, Sloan, and Pearce, 1932) and *The Gathering of Zion: The Story of the Mormon Trail* (New York: McGraw-Hill, 1964).

7. *Sound of Mountain Water*, 32.

8. Sid Jenson, "The Compassionate Seer: Wallace Stegner as Literary Artist," *Critical Essays on Wallace Stegner*, Anthony Arthur, ed. (Boston: G. K. Hall, 1982), 164–75.

9. Robert Canzoneri, "Wallace Stegner: Trial by Existence [The Shorter Works]," *Critical Essays*, 67.

10. "Henry Adams, Wallace Stegner, and the Search for a Sense of Place in the West," *Critical Essays*, 94.

11. "Western Fiction and History: a Reconsideration," *Critical Essays*, 152.

12. Wendell Berry and Mindy Weintraub, "A Question a Day: A Written Conversation with Wendell Berry," *Wendell Berry*, American Authors Series, Paul Merchant, ed. (Lewiston, Idaho: Confluence Press, 1991), 41.

13. "Wallace Stegner and the Great Community," *What Are People For?*, 50.

14. Edward Abbey admired these qualities in Berry's life and work, writing about Berry that he "is not only a good novelist and poet, but a brilliant essayist, able to combine clear thinking, strong language, and comprehensive ideas in a sure, graceful, wholly unified style. See *The Unsettling of America* or *The Long-Legged House* for powerful examples of what I mean. On top of that, Berry has been successful in teaching, farming, and most difficult of all, in marriage; he actually lives what he preaches, which seems grossly unfair to the rest of us; how can we forgive him his happiness?" (*AR*, xx–xxi).

15. *Wendell Berry*, 60.

16. "V," *Sabbaths* (San Francisco: North Point Press, 1987), 88–89.

17. *Home Economics: Fourteen Essays by Wendell Berry* (San Francisco: North Point Press, 1988), 15, 20.

18. *Crossing Open Ground* (New York: Vintage Books, 1988), 69.

19. *For the Love of the World*, 78.

20. *Crossing Open Ground*, 64–65, 68.

21. *The Rediscovery of North America* (New York: Vintage Books, 1990), 36.

22. Jim Anton, "An Interview with Barry Lopez," *Western American Literature*, 21 (1) (May 1986): 17.

23. "Dialogue One: Ecology and the Human Imagination, Barry Lopez and Edward O. Wilson," *Writing Natural History: Dialogues with*

Authors, Edward Lueders, ed., (Salt Lake City: University of Utah Press, 1989), 22, 16, 27. For Lopez's regard for Abbey, see his "Meeting Ed Abbey," in *RM*, 67–70.

24. *Crossing Open Ground,* 71, 200.

25. *Rediscovery of North America,* 31.

26. "Dialogue Two: Landscape, People, and Place, Robert Finch and Terry Tempest Williams," *Writing Natural History,* 41.

27. *Writing Natural History,* 46, 62. Terry Williams's own volume of essays, *Refuge: An Unnatural History of Family and Place* (New York: Vintage Books, 1991), places her among these writers. In it she movingly interweaves discussions of feminist politics, family crises, and spiritual matters with discussions of natural history and environmental issues.

Bibliography

Abbey, Edward. *Abbey's Road*. New York: E.P. Dutton, 1979.

Abbey, Edward. *Beyond the Wall: Essays from the Outside*. New York: Holt Rinehart & Winston, 1984.

Abbey, Edward. *The Brave Cowboy: An Old Tale in a New Time*. Albuquerque: University of New Mexico Press, 1956.

Abbey, Edward. *Desert Solitaire: A Season in the Wilderness*. New York: McGraw-Hill, 1968.

Abbey, Edward. *Down the River*. New York: E.P. Dutton, 1982.

Abbey, Edward. *The Fool's Progress (an Honest Novel)*. New York: Henry Holt, 1988.

Abbey, Edward. *Good News*. New York: E.P. Dutton, 1980.

Abbey, Edward. *Hayduke Lives!* Boston: Little, Brown, 1990.

Abbey, Edward. *The Journey Home: Some Words in Defense of the American West*. New York: E.P. Dutton, 1977.

Abbey, Edward. *The Monkey Wrench Gang*. New York: Avon Books, 1975.

Abbey, Edward. *One Life at a Time, Please*. New York: Henry Holt, 1988.

Abbey, Edward. *A Voice Crying in the Wilderness: (Vox Clamantis in Deserto), Notes from a Secret Journal*. New York: St. Martin's Press, 1990.

Arthur, Anthony, ed. *Critical Essays on Wallace Stegner*. Boston: G.K. Hall, 1982.

Baumann, Michael. *B. Traven: An Introduction*. Albuquerque: University of New Mexico Press, 1976.

Berry, Wendell. *Collected Poems 1957–1982*. San Francisco: North Point Press, 1985.

Berry, Wendell. *A Continuous Harmony: Essays Cultural and Agricultural*. New York: Harcourt Brace Jovanovich, 1972.

Berry, Wendell. *The Gift of Good Land: Further Essays Cultural and Agricultural*. San Francisco: North Point Press, 1981.

Berry, Wendell. *Home Economics: Fourteen Essays*. San Francisco: North Point Press, 1988.

Berry, Wendell. *The Long-Legged House*. New York: Harcourt Brace Jovanovich, 1969.

Berry, Wendell. *Standing by Words: Essays by Wendell Berry*. San Francisco: North Point Press, 1983.

Berry, Wendell. *The Unsettling of America: Culture and Agriculture*. San Francisco: Sierra Club Books, 1977.

Botkin, Daniel B. *Discordant Harmonies: A New Ecology for the Twenty-first Century*. New York, Oxford University Press, 1990.

Bowler, Peter J. *Evolution: The History of an Idea*. Berkeley: University of California Press, 1984.

Brooks, Paul. *Speaking for Nature: How Literary Naturalists from Henry David Thoreau to Rachel Carson Have Shaped America*. Boston: Houghton Mifflin, 1980.

Callicott, J. Baird, ed. *Companion to* A Sand County Almanac: *Interpretive and Critical Essays*. Madison: University of Wisconsin Press, 1987.

Dillard, Annie. *An American Childhood*. New York: Harper & Row, 1987.

Dillard, Annie. *Holy the Firm*. New York: Bantam Books, 1977.

Dillard, Annie. *The Living*. New York: Harper Collins, 1992.

Dillard, Annie. *Pilgrim at Tinker Creek: A Mystical Excursion into the Natural World*. New York: Bantam Books, 1974.

Dillard, Annie. *Teaching a Stone to Talk: Expeditions and Encounters*. New York: Harper & Row, 1982.

Elder, John. *Imagining the Earth: Poetry and the Vision of Nature*. Urbana: University of Illinois Press, 1985.

Elton, Charles. *Animal Ecology*. With an introduction by Julian S. Huxley. New York: Macmillan, 1927.

Evans, Mary Alice and Howard Ensign Evans. *William Morton Wheeler, Biologist*. Cambridge: Harvard University Press, 1970.

Finch, Robert, and John Elder, eds. *The Norton Book of Nature Writing*. New York: W. W. Norton, 1990.

Flader, Susan L.. *Thinking Like a Mountain: Aldo Leopold and the Evolution of an Ecological Attitude toward Deer, Wolves, and Forests*. Columbia: University of Missouri Press, 1974.

Flader, Susan L., and J. Baird Callicott, eds. *The River of the Mother of God and Other Essays by Aldo Leopold*. Madison: University of Wisconsin Press, 1991.

Foreman, Dave, and Bill Haywood, eds. *Ecodefense: A Field Guide to Monkeywrenching*. 2d ed. Tucson: Nedd Ludd Book, 1987.

Fox, Stephen R. *John Muir and His Legacy: The American Conservation Movement*. Boston: Little, Brown, 1981. Reprint: *The American Con-*

servation Movement: John Muir and His Legacy. Madison: University of Wisconsin Press, 1986.

Fritzell, Peter A. *Nature Writing and America: Essays upon a Cultural Type*. Ames: Iowa State University Press, 1990.

Griffin, Donald R. *Animal Minds*. Chicago: University of Chicago Press, 1992.

Griffin, Donald R. *Animal Thinking*. Cambridge: Harvard University Press, 1984.

Griffin, Donald R. *The Question of Animal Awareness: Evolutionary Continuity of Mental Experience*. New York: Rockefeller University Press, 1976.

Halper, Jon, ed. *Gary Snyder: Dimensions of a Life*. San Francisco: Sierra Club Books, 1991.

Halpern, Daniel, ed. *On Nature: Nature, Landscape, and Natural History*. San Francisco: North Point Press, 1987.

Hepworth, James, and Gregory McNamee, eds. *Resist Much, Obey Little: Some Notes on Edward Abbey*. Salt Lake City: Dream Garden Press, 1985.

Jeffers, Robinson. *Cawdor and Other Poems*. New York: Horace Liveright, 1928.

Jeffers, Robinson. *The Double Axe and Other Poems*. New York: Random House, 1948.

Jeffers, Robinson. *Roan Stallion, Tamar, and Other Poems*. New York: Modern Library, 1935.

Jeffers, Robinson. *The Selected Poetry of Robinson Jeffers*. New York: Random House, 1935.

Krutch, Joseph Wood. *The Best Nature Writing of Joseph Wood Krutch*. New York, William Morrow, 1969.

Krutch, Joseph Wood. *The Desert Year*. New York: William Sloane, 1952.

Krutch, Joseph Wood. *The Forgotten Peninsula: A Naturalist in Baja California*. New York, William Sloane, 1961.

Krutch, Joseph Wood. *Grand Canyon: Today and All Its Yesterdays*. New York, William Sloane, 1958.

Krutch, Joseph Wood. *Great American Nature Writing*. New York: William Sloane, 1950.

Krutch, Joseph Wood. *The Great Chain of Life*. Boston: Houghton Mifflin, 1956.

Krutch, Joseph Wood. *Henry David Thoreau*. American Men of Letters Series. New York: William Sloane, 1948.

Krutch, Joseph Wood. *If You Don't Mind My Saying So: Essays on Man and Nature*. New York: William Sloane, 1965.

Krutch, Joseph Wood. *A Krutch Omnibus: Forty Years of Social and Literary Criticism.* New York: William Morrow, 1970.

Krutch, Joseph Wood. *The Measure of Man: On Freedom, Human Values, Survival and the Modern Temper.* Indianapolis: Bobbs Merrill, 1954.

Krutch, Joseph Wood. *The Modern Temper: A Study and a Confession.* 1929. Reprint. New York: Harcourt, Brace & World, 1956.

Krutch, Joseph Wood. *More Lives Than One.* New York: William Sloane, 1962.

Krutch, Joseph Wood. *The Twelve Seasons: A Perpetual Calendar for the Country.* New York, William Sloane, 1949.

Krutch, Joseph Wood. *The Voice of the Desert: A Naturalist's Interpretation.* New York: William Sloane, 1955.

Leopold, Aldo. *Game Management.* New York: Scribner's, 1933. Reprint. Madison: University of Wisconsin Press, 1986.

Leopold, Aldo. *A Sand County Almanac: With Essays on Conservation from Round River.* New York: Oxford University Press, 1966.

Lopez, Barry. *Arctic Dreams: Imagination and Desire in a Northern Landscape.* New York: Bantam Books, 1986.

Lopez, Barry. *Crossing Open Ground.* New York: Vintage Books, 1988.

Lopez, Barry. *The Rediscovery of North America.* New York: Vintage Books, 1990.

Lueders, Edward, ed. *Writing Natural History: Dialogues with Authors.* Salt Lake City: University of Utah Press, 1989.

Lyon, Thomas J., ed. *This Incomperable Lande: A Book of American Nature Writing.* Boston: Houghton Mifflin, 1989.

McClintock, James I. *White Logic: Jack London's Short Stories.* Grand Rapids, Mich.: Wolf House Books, 1975.

McIntosh, Robert P. *The Background of Ecology: Concept and Theory.* New York: Cambridge University Press, 1985.

Margalef, Ramon. *Perspectives in Ecological Theory.* Chicago: University of Chicago Press, 1968.

Margolis, John D. *Joseph Wood Krutch: A Writer's Life.* Knoxville: University of Tennessee Press, 1980.

Meine, Curt. *Aldo Leopold: His Life and Work.* Madison: University of Wisconsin Press, 1988.

Molesworth, Charles. *Gary Snyder's Vision: Poetry and the Real Work.* Columbia: University of Missouri Press, 1983.

Morgan, Ann Haven. *Field Book of Ponds and Streams: An Introduction to the Life of Fresh Water.* New York: Putnam's, 1930.

Nash, Roderick Frazier. *The Rights of Nature: A History of Environmental Ethics.* Madison: University of Wisconsin Press, 1989.

Nash, Roderick. *Wilderness and the American Mind*. New Haven: Yale University Press, 1967.

Oates, David. *Earth Rising: Ecological Belief in an Age of Science*. Corvallis: Oregon State University Press, 1989.

Odum, Eugene P. *Fundamentals of Ecology*. New York: Holt, Rinehart and Winston, 1963.

Odum, Howard T. *Environment, Power and Society*. New York: Wiley-Interscience, 1971.

Oelschlaeger, Max. *The Idea of Wilderness from Prehistory to the Age of Ecology*. New Haven: Yale University Press, 1991.

Passmore, John. *Man's Responsibility for Nature: Ecological Problems and Western Traditions*. New York: Scribner, 1974.

Paul, Sherman. *For the Love of the World: Essays on Nature Writers*. Iowa City: University of Iowa Press, 1992.

Petulla, Joseph M. *American Environmentalism: Values, Tactics, Priorities*. College Station: Texas A & M University Press, 1980.

Pinchot, Gifford. *The Fight for Conservation*. New York: Doubleday, Page 1910.

Ronald, Ann. *The New West of Edward Abbey*. Albuquerque: University of New Mexico Press, 1982.

Sale, Kirkpatrick. *Dwellers in the Land: The Bioregional Vision*. San Francisco: Sierra Club Books, 1985.

Slovic, Scott. *Seeking Awareness in American Nature Writing: Henry Thoreau, Annie Dillard, Edward Abbey, Wendell Berry, Barry Lopez*. Salt Lake City: University of Utah Press, 1992.

Snyder, Gary. *Axe Handles*. San Francisco: North Point Press, 1983.

Snyder, Gary. *Earth House Hold*. New York: New Directions, 1969.

Snyder, Gary. *Left Out in the Rain: New Poems 1947–1985*. San Francisco, North Point Press, 1986.

Snyder, Gary. *Myths & Texts*. New York: Totem Press, 1960.

Snyder, Gary. *No Nature: New and Selected Poems*. New York: Pantheon Books, 1992.

Snyder, Gary. *The Old Ways: Six Essays*. San Francisco: City Lights Books, 1977.

Snyder, Gary. *The Practice of the Wild*. San Francisco: North Point Press, 1990.

Snyder, Gary. *The Real Work: Interviews & Talks 1974–1979*. William Scott McLean, ed. New York: New Directions, 1980.

Snyder, Gary. *Regarding Wave*. New York: New Directions, 1967.

Snyder, Gary. *Turtle Island*. New York: New Directions Books, 1974.

Stegner, Wallace. *Angle of Repose*. Garden City, N.Y.: Doubleday, 1971.

Stegner, Wallace. *Beyond the Hundredth Meridian: John Wesley Powell and the Second Opening of the West*. Boston: Houghton Mifflin, 1954.

Stegner, Wallace. *The Big Rock Candy Mountain*. New York: Duell, Sloan, and Pearce, 1943.

Stegner, Wallace. *The Sound of Mountain Water*. Garden City, N.Y.: Doubleday, 1969.

Stegner, Wallace. *Where the Bluebird Sings to the Lemonade Springs: Living and Writing in the West*. New York: Random House, 1992.

Stegner, Wallace. *Willow: A History, a Story, and a Memory of the Last Plains Frontier*. New York: Viking, 1962.

Stegner, Wallace, and Richard Etulain. *Conversations with Wallace Stegner*. Salt Lake City: University of Utah Press, 1984.

Steuding, Bob. *Gary Snyder*. Boston: Twayne, 1976.

Thoreau, Henry David. *Walden*. J. Lyndon Shanley, ed. Princeton: Princeton University Press, 1973.

Trimble, Stephen, ed. *Words from the Land: Encounters with Natural History Writing*. Salt Lake City: Peregrine Smith, 1988.

Wheeler, William Morton. *Essays in Philosophical Biology*. Cambridge: Harvard University Press, 1970.

Worster, Donald. *Nature's Economy: The Roots of Ecology*. San Francisco: Sierra Club Books, 1977.

Worster, Donald, ed. *American Environmentalism: The Formative Period, 1860–1915*. New York: Wiley, 1973.

Index

Abbey, Edward, 88 89, 98, 108, 109, 144; ecological biology, 3; and Thoreauvian Romanticism, 3, 4, 16, 67, 68, 73–74, 75; Thoreau's influence on, 4, 6–7, 84; science in, 4, 7, 12, 16, 19, 73; Krutch's influence on, 6, 65–66, 67, 68; as anarchist, 7, 17, 18, 66, 69, 81–85, 87; compared to Dillard, 8, 16, 87; compared to Krutch, 16, 65, 66, 72, 87; world view, 16, 73; environmentalism, 18; despair and isolation, 18, 67, 69, 70–72, 80, 82, 87, 105; mysticism, 18, 73, 75, 79; 'mystery' of nature, 18, 157n2,; joy in nature, 20, 60, 66, 67; the desert southwest, 20, 71, 74, 146; metabiology, 66; and religion, 66; conversion experience, 66, 67, 69, 71, 74–75, 79; humor of, 66, 82, 83, 84, 85, 86; spiritual complexity, 66–67; death, 67; early years, 67; "Earthiest," 67, 74, 87; place in writers' lineage, 67–69, 86; Whitman's influence on, 69, 86; identifies with London, 69–75, 79, 86; wilderness mythos, 70; Darwinian nature, 72–73; as biocentrist, 74–75, 84, 87; Inhumanism, 75–76, 79, 83, 86; compared to Jeffers, 75–79; nihilism, 77, 79, 83, 86;

technology, 78; visionary, 78, 79; Traven's influence on, 80–87; Stegner's influence on, 131; on Berry, 161n14. *See also Desert Solitaire*; Earth First!; Kindred Spirits; *Monkey Wrench Gang*

Adams, Ansel, 89

Affirmation, 17, 71, 72, 79, 93, 94, 99, 102, 107, 142. *See also* Conversion experience

Alaska, 70, 74

Alexander, Samuel, 57

Algren, Nelson, 86

Alienation, 51. *See also* Conversion Experience

Ammons, A. R., 10, 65, 95, 127

Anarchy, 146; theorist Kropotkin, 17; Earth First!, 18; Traven, 80, 81–83; anarchist comedy, 81–82, 85, 86. *See also* Abbey, Edward

Anthropocentrism, 3, 5, 31, 32, 38, 48; Leopold, 5; compared with Biocentrism, 11, 74; "Abrahamic" stance, 30, 37–38; Lynn White, Jr., 38; 89; Abbey, 74

Anthropology, 21, 43, 109, 111, 119, 124, 142, 144, 145

Anthropomorphism, 58, 59

Arcadian Tradition: influenced Thoreau, 10; in essays, 10–11

Arctic regions, 98, 142

Arizona: Abbey in, 20; influenced